ISBN 978-0-266-15801-1
PIBN 10037981

This book is a reproduction of an important historical work. Forgotten Books uses
state-of-the-art technology to digitally reconstruct the work, preserving the original format
whilst repairing imperfections present in the aged copy. In rare cases, an imperfection in
the original, such as a blemish or missing page, may be replicated in our edition. We do,
however, repair the vast majority of imperfections successfully; any imperfections that
remain are intentionally left to preserve the state of such historical works.

MUNICIPAL BOOK-KEEPING

BY

J. H. McCALL, F.S.A.A.

BOROUGH ACCOUNTANT, COUNTY BOROUGH OF CROYDON;
FELLOW OF THE SOCIETY OF INCORPORATED ACCOUNTANTS
AND AUDITORS (FIRST PLACE FINAL EXAMINATIONS,
1907); FELLOW OF THE INSTITUTE OF MUNICIPAL
TREASURERS AND ACCOUNTANTS

LONDON
SIR ISAAC PITMAN & SONS, LTD.
PARKER STREET, KINGSWAY, W.C.2
BATH, MELBOURNE, TORONTO, NEW YORK
1921

PREFACE

" Wherever thou findest Disorder, there is thy eternal enemy;
attack him swiftly, subdue him; make Order of him, the subject not of Chaos, but of Intelligence, Divinity and Thee. The
thistle that grows in thy path, dig it out."—CARLYLE, "*Past and
Present.*"

UNDER the influence of that noble book from which the
above quotation is made, I first conceived book-keeping
as a task of bringing order out of confusion. The thistle
to be dug out, grew, of course, in my own mind, as it does
in the mind of any student. A friend placed into my
hands the first book on book-keeping I had ever seen; it
was one of Pitman's publications—*Book-keeping Simplified*—
and I shall ever remain grateful for the help I got from
that little book.

A large proportion of books written on the general
subject of book-keeping contains an abundance of forms,
detailed exercises and footnotes. I have as far as possible
kept to the plain attempt to state reasons for the
application of rules, and I would particularly emphasize
the importance of reading the first two chapters as the
basis of the succeeding chapters.

My object has been to produce a book for junior
municipal book-keepers which may be helpful to them in
their daily work, and which may be of some service to
those studying for the examinations of the Institute of
Municipal Treasurers and Accountants.

I have not hesitated to state my own opinions on many
things which are considered by some as controversial,
as I have very good evidence for believing that the same
methods of applying the principles of book-keeping
obtaining in the commercial world will ultimately be
applied to all accounts of Local Authorities.

J. H. M.

CONTENTS

CHAPTER IV

THE RATING FUNDS

CHAPTER V

THE TRADING UNDERTAKINGS

CHAPTER VI

CAPITAL OR LOAN EXPENDITURE

CHAPTER VII

THE ISSUE OF STOCK AND ITS REDEMPTION

CHAPTER VIII

MISCELLANEOUS FUNDS

CHAPTER IX

STORES RECORDS AND COST ACCOUNTS

Stores Records

Cost Accounts

CHAPTER X

ACCOUNTANCY PROBLEMS

CHAPTER XI

MODERN DEVICES FOR BOOK-KEEPING

CHAPTER XII

THE EXAMINATION OF THE INSTITUTE OF MUNICIPAL TREASURERS AND ACCOUNTANTS

APPENDIX

ERRATA

Page 57. (4) Rent chargeable to tenants.
—This should read, " The Local Authority in first fixing the rents under an assisted scheme may have regard to the rents obtaining in the locality for houses, for the working classes, and to the operation of the Increase of Rent and Mortgage Interest (War Restrictions) Act, 1915, and any Acts amending or extending that Act : but in that case the Local Authorities should also have regard to—

(*a*) any increase of rents authorized by any such Acts ; and

(*b*) any superiority in the condition or amenity of the houses to be let by them under the assisted scheme or in the accommodation provided therein."

Page 68. 1. (*c*) should read—" the prevention of misappropriation of material."

(1763)

sh Basis " of keeping
pal Accounts.
come and Expendi-
basis.
s and extensions of
oks of Account.
ation of Books.
or the Book-keeper.

ig.

its widest sense
sactions involving
: many methods
ing, whilst others,
: useful for their
developed upon
book-keeping is
ng to attain the
ı be applicable in

The object of book-keeping should be to record the transactions in a systematic manner in order that—

(*a*) The accuracy of the entries may be proved.

(*b*) Periodical results may be obtained classified in the particular form required.

(*c*) The true financial position may be readily ascertained at any time.

CHAPTE

THE EXAMINATION OF THE
TREASURERS AN

APPEN

MUNICIPAL BOOK-KEEPING

CHAPTER I

BOOK-KEEPING

(1) The Objects of Book-keeping.

THE term " Book-keeping " is used in its widest sense to denote any method of recording transactions involving money or money's worth. There are many methods still in use which are faulty and misleading, whilst others, though unscientific, may still be quite useful for their purpose. Modern methods have been developed upon definite principles and in this relation book-keeping is defined as a " science," the object being to attain the results required by a system which may be applicable in theory to all kinds of accounts.

The object of book-keeping should be to record the transactions in a systematic manner in order that—

(a) The accuracy of the entries may be proved.

(b) Periodical results may be obtained classified in the particular form required.

(c) The true financial position may be readily ascertained at any time.

1—(1763)

(2) The Theory of Double Entry.

The system known as *Double entry* book-keeping is acknowledged to be sufficient for the attainment of these objects. This system is based upon the fact that a transaction between two persons has a twofold aspect which can be recorded, viz., the transfer of money or money's worth involving a giver and a receiver. Many transactions require as many as four entries to be made, therefore the term "double entry" must not be taken to mean "two entries." Nothing can be more erroneous than to define double entry book-keeping as the method of recording transactions by debiting one account and crediting another. Part of the system is the use of two columns for every account, the one on the left-hand side being called the "Debit" and the one on the right-hand side the "Credit" column. The words "Debit" and "Credit" are understood in all cases to mean either addition or subtraction. To deduct the total of one column from the total of the other column will give the same result as adding or deducting each item where one column is used.

(3) The Classification of Accounts.

Accounts may be classified as follows—

(*a*) PERSONAL ACCOUNTS. These as the name signifies are the accounts which show the sums due to or from individuals, firms and corporations.

(*b*) REAL ACCOUNTS. These are sometimes called "Property" accounts and are supposed to deal with material things as Cash, Goods, Buildings, Fixtures, etc.

(*c*) NOMINAL ACCOUNTS. These may be taken to include all accounts which cannot be classified as Personal or Real. The chief accounts are those relating to Expenses, Profit and Loss, etc.

(4) The Primary Books of Account.

Originally all entries were written into a *Journal* and posted therefrom to the respective accounts which were kept in a book called the *Ledger*. These two books have been divided and sub-divided to meet the necessities of trade and the volume of business. The Cash Account is kept in a separate book, Personal and Nominal Ledgers are used for their respective classes of accounts. This process of sub-division has produced an extraordinary number of books with different titles in different businesses ; it will be shown later that the various books used in the finance office of a local authority are but divisions of the Cash Book, the Ledger, or the Journal.

(5) The Rules for Posting by Double Entry.

Transactions are entered to the debit or credit of their respective accounts subject to the following rules.

RULE 1.—Applicable to Personal Accounts. Debit the receiver ; credit the giver.

RULE 2.—Applicable to Real Accounts. Debit what comes in ; credit what goes out.

RULE 3.—Applicable to Nominal Accounts. Debit expenses and losses ; credit gains.

It will be seen that a transaction will affect two accounts, *e.g.*, to record the receipt of goods from Jones it is necessary to debit goods with what comes in according to rule and to credit the giver Jones. The effect of thus posting all entries according to their twofold aspect is that "every debit has a corresponding credit" and in consequence "the total of the debts must equal the total of the credits."

(6) The Results to be Obtained from Double Entry.

Assuming that all the transactions for a certain period have been posted to the proper accounts it will be possible to obtain the desired objects of a good system as under.

FIRST to prove the books. The accounts are cast, and the balances taken to a summary of debits and credits called the Trial Balance. If the total of the debits agrees with the total of the credits the books are said to be proved. It must be pointed out, however, that other errors may exist which are not disclosed by the Trial Balance, *e.g.*, where both a credit and its debit have not been posted, or where an account has been wrongly debited or credited.

SECOND to ascertain the results. This is done by gathering all expenses, losses and gains arising out of the transactions within the period into an account called the Profit and Loss or Revenue Account. If this results in a debit balance there is said to be a Loss or Deficiency, if a credit balance a Profit or Surplus.

THIRD to show the Financial Position. This is done by grouping and classifying all the balances which remain in the books after transfers or closing entries have been made and stating them in the form of a *Balance Sheet*. The debit balances are shown on the right-hand side and are generally described under the heading of *Assets*. The credits are taken to the left hand side under the heading of *Liabilities*. Some accounts, however, do not lend themselves to being placed under either the heading of Assets or Liabilities, and it is important to bear in mind that each sub-heading or description should be sufficient to prevent any misunderstanding. The excess of what are called the Assets over the Liabilities in a trader's account is represented by the balance to the credit of his Capital Account.   .

(7) The " Cash Basis " of Keeping Municipal Accounts.

The principles of double entry outlined above may be applied to the account keeping of any business or undertaking. Short cuts may be made without seriously infringing the rules, but the student should thoroughly understand the rules first. The accounts of Local Authorities are generally supposed to be kept upon the principle of double entry. It is within the province of every student to test whether this is so. There are two phrases familiar to municipal book-keepers which are used in relation to the accounts of Local Authorities— " keeping the accounts on a cash basis " and " keeping the accounts on Income and Expenditure lines." The *cash basis* in its simplest form is the record in a cash book of all cash received and paid during some period. So far the rules of double entry are not observed. The Ministry of Health, however, requires a summary of the cash items in the annual financial statement for Urban District Councils. In order to give the information required, it is necessary to analyse the items under certain heads of expenditure. This is done by posting the cash entries to a book with accounts as specified in the return. This looks very like double entry. The result obtained is an analysis of the cash transactions summarized in a statement, the balance of which corresponds to the cash in hand or overdrawn. The financial position of the Local Authority is not disclosed, no account being taken of moneys owing by or due to them. It will be seen that the objects of a good system are far from being attained.

(8) The " Income and Expenditure " Basis.

An attempt is sometimes made to remedy the obvious defects of the " cash system " by tacking on at the end of the year the outstanding liabilities and income. This is done by debiting in the ledger in its respective account each item of Expenditure and crediting a personal account in the Creditors Ledger. The income is added to the analysed receipts and debited to the personal accounts in the Debtors Ledger. In the new year the creditors are closed by posting the payments relating thereto from the cash book, and the debtors cleared by posting the receipts relating to each account. The personal accounts under this method are introduced at the end of the year and closed in the new year, when the cash is received or paid, but after such closing they remain dead until the next balancing time.

Both the methods of book-keeping described have been defended on the ground that the Ministry of Health does not require more than an analysis of cash, and that the result attained by keeping personal accounts does not justify the labour entailed. In commercial accounts much more could be said in defence of the system known as " single entry." The student is asked to apply the scientific tests—first, as to how far the three main objects of book-keeping are attained, and secondly, whether the three golden rules of double entry are observed. He will then be in a position to judge for himself whether they are worthy of being included in that definition which defines book-keeping as the " *science* of recording transactions, etc."

No system is worthy of the name which does not provide for income and expenditure, and it cannot be called the double entry system unless it does so. If every entry is made relating to the transactions within the period, then all expenditure will be recorded, including, of course, apportionment of contracts which were partly completed at the date of the Balance Sheet. Income will also include everything earned within the period both due and accrued.

(9) Variations and Extensions of the Books of Account.

Owing to the bulk of the transactions and the peculiar nature of each business or undertaking, it is necessary to make variations in the primary books of account. This is done in two ways—

FIRST, BY EXPANSION. This is effected by a sub-division

of the books. The cash book may be split into two parts—the Cash Payments Book and the Cash Receipts Book. The Ledger can be divided according to the classification of accounts as follows : (1) Creditors Ledger and Debtors Ledger for personal accounts ; (2) Revenue Ledger, Capital Ledger, and so on, for nominal accounts. No difficulty will be experienced in recognizing these sub-divisions, owing to their character. The Journal can be sub-divided into a number of books of original entry, which unfortunately are not always called the same names. In a municipality we have the Income Journals, the Expenditure Journal (sometimes called the Invoice Book or the Orders on Borough Treasurer Book) and various other Day Books. It must be borne in mind that all these books of original entry from which debit and credit postings are made are records of income or expenditure, and further, that they form part of the book known as the Journal. Understood in this sense the Journal is always used. Questions on the use of the Journal frequently refer to that portion of it which should be reserved for transfers, closing entries, etc.

SECONDLY, BY CONTRACTION. This is generally effected by the use of the columnar system. We will assume the Authority owns Gas, Electricity and Tramways Undertakings. Instead of using the three cash books, one may be adapted by the use of four columns, a total column and one column for each undertaking into which the receipts or payments are extended. Debtors may be entered in rotation with the columns extended for all possible entries. A good example of this is the Rate Book or Gas Rental. Here again the book-keeper should know the class of account he is occupied upon in order to learn the general system.

There are many practical variations in addition to the above, but in adopting them no rule in double entry book-keeping need be broken. It is sometimes convenient to adopt what is known as the *Card System* for personal accounts or even cost accounts, this being merely a variation from the form of the bound book.

A system known as *Slip Book-keeping* is frequently used in commercial houses. The practice is to attach numbered slips to the sale notes, from which the debit entry is made direct to the Debtors Ledger, and the credit entry to the Sales Account. The slips themselves take the place of the Journal or Day Book. *Loose Leaf Ledgers* are a departure from the form of bound ledger, and are recognized as being useful for arranging the accounts in some convenient order, alphabetical or otherwise ; and for the elimination of dead accounts. They are being introduced into the offices of all large municipalities despite academic objections.

(10) Organization of Books.

The objects to be borne in mind in organizing a system of books are—

(*a*) The particular requirements of the business.

(*b*) The best results for the labour involved.

(*c*) The ready reference to the records.

(*d*) To ensure the highest degree of clerical accuracy.

(*e*) To provide safeguards against frauds.

It is not intended in this volume to discuss the problems of office organization. It will be sufficient to say that the books should be so designed that the members of the staff are able to form some check upon each other's work.

(11) Rules for the Book-keeper.

The best systems will fail unless the book-keeper is trained to his work. There are one or two rules for him, the observance of which are essential to obtain good results.

(*a*) The narration of each transaction should be sufficient to explain it without relying upon the memory. This is sufficient if contained in one book, and the details need not be duplicated in the contra entries. The point to remember is, sufficiency of detail without unnecessary duplication.

(b) All transactions should be recorded as soon as practicable. The date of the entry should also be the date of the transaction. It is convenient, however, for accounts to be entered up after approval by the Committee, as on the date of the Committee ; but at the end of the year no entries relating to the financial year should be dated after 31st March, although not passed by the Committee until after the close of the financial year.

(c) In order to localize errors and save time when balancing, all the books should be made self-balancing. In order to do this it is necessary to construct *Total Accounts* for each ledger, which should be under the control of the chief book-keeper. The method of splitting the Rate Book into portions representing Collecting Districts, and balancing each portion separately is no doubt familiar. In order to do this an analysis is kept of the rate made, the cash collected, and amounts written off. In the same way Total Accounts may be prepared in respect of any ledgers, and for the sake of illustration we may take the Creditors Ledger. This would be constructed on the following lines—

Debit Side—

(a) Total of the opening debit balances, if any.

(b) Cash paid ; the total of the cash book relating to that ledger.

(c) Transfers and other items extracted and analyzed from the Journal.

Credit Side—

(a) Total of the opening balances.

(b) Goods purchased ; the total of the invoice book or Purchases Journal.

(c) Transfers and other items extracted and analyzed from the Journal.

The balance on this total account should then be the same as the total of the balances when extracted from the Creditors Ledger.

If the Total Accounts are kept for all ledgers then the debit and credit balances of such accounts should agree. This is important to remember, as errors are sometimes made in preparing the Total Accounts, and much time wasted in trying to find such errors in the ledgers.

CHAPTER II

BOOK-KEEPING APPLIED TO MUNICIPAL ACCOUNTS

1. General considerations.
2. The preparation of Rate and other Estimates.
3. The control over the Expenditure of Committees.
4. The requirements of Government Departments.
5. The preparation of Accounts for Audit.
6. The annual Abstract of Accounts.
7. The organization of the Account Keeping.
8. The Allocation and Dissection of Accounts.

(1) General Considerations.

THE methods of account keeping by Local Authorities are varied. This is due to the fact that there are several classes of authorities—Rural Districts, Urban Districts, Non-County Boroughs, County Boroughs, and County Councils, etc., each having different powers and duties. Attempts have been made to standardize the form of accounts, but so long as inherent defects remain in the old methods this would always be unsatisfactory. A difficulty to be overcome is the local enthusiasm which may develop the activities of a particular corporation in the direction of optional powers. The steady increase of powers and duties demands a system which has elasticity. Apart from the foregoing there are many considerations to be taken into account which are general to all Local Authorities. The book-keeping should be arranged to provide certain necessary information required for various purposes.

(2) The Preparation of Rate and Other Estimates.

The Local Authority has been created by statute mainly for the purpose of rendering services to the community. The expenses are chargeable generally to two funds,

11

the General District and the Borough Fund. The charge
for such services is levied upon the inhabitants of the
district by means of certain rates. Such rates are made
half-yearly or annually upon the estimate of the expenditure
for the period for which the rate is made. The estimate
is a forecast of what is likely to be spent, and is based
largely upon the actual expenditure of the preceding
year. The estimates are prepared in detail and grouped
generally according to the particular services controlled
by each Committee of the Council. It will be seen,
therefore, that the book-keeping must be adapted for
the purpose of furnishing the details of actual income and
expenditure in the form required for the estimates.

(3) The Control over the Expenditure of Committees.

The standing orders of the Council usually set out the
duties of each committee and the matters over which
they have control. Their expenditure is supposed to be
limited by the amounts provided for in the estimates.
Expenditure not so provided for is generally sanctioned
subject to the consent of the Finance Committee. The
duty of the Financial Officer is to watch all expenditure
and report periodically to the committees, as to whether
they are over-spent or not. The books therefore should
be so framed that not only can the expenditure under the
various estimate headings in detail be ascertained at the
end of the financial year, but at any interim period.

(4) The Requirements of Government Departments.

The Ministry of Health requires certain information at
the end of each financial year embodied in the following
returns—

(a) The Financial Statement. This was originally,
and is now in the case of small authorities, a summary of

receipts and payments of all authorities who are subject
to audit by the District Auditor, *viz.*, Rural and Urban
Districts, Metropolitan Boroughs, County Councils and
certain Municipal Boroughs.   It has been modified in the
case of the Metropolitan Boroughs and larger Urban
Districts to contain a summary of income and expenditure.

(*b*) The Financial Statement for all Local Education
Authorities.   Like (*a*) it is adapted in many cases to
contain income and expenditure.

(*c*) The Statement for Boroughs not subject to the
District Auditor known as the " A and B " Return.   This
provides for the information to be based upon receipts
and payments but no objection is made to its being utilized
for income and expenditure.

(*d*) The Sinking Funds and Loan Statements of Boroughs
who have Stock Issues, and Returns to Public Works Loan
Commissioners.

(*e*) The accounts and Balance Sheets of certain Trading
Undertakings required by the Board of Trade.   The
published Abstract of Accounts of the authority is
generally accepted now.

In the preparation of these returns a difficulty arises by
reason of the divisions of expenditure being different to the
grouping of the details required for the Committees and
for the estimates.   This must be taken into account when
instituting a system of allocation and analysis.

In addition to the above returns the Ministry of Health
requires specific information in all cases where grants are
made based upon a proportion of the expenditure.

The following are instances—

(*a*) Maternity and Child Welfare.

(*b*) Treatment of Tuberculosis.

(*c*) Treatment of Venereal Disease.

(*d*) Food Control.

(*e*) Household Fuel Order.

(*f*) Mental Deficiency Act, 1913.

Claims for grants are made on the prescribed forms and in the case of disputes the actual vouchers supporting the claim are sometimes required to be sent to the Ministry of Health.

(5) The Preparation of Accounts for Audit.

The accounts of Local Authorities are subject to audit by specified persons as follows—

(a) Municipal Boroughs. Two Elective and one Mayor's Auditor for all accounts except Education, Food Control and Housing (assisted schemes). In addition professional auditors are often employed under powers given either in Local Acts or under section 19 of the Municipal Corporations Act, 1882.

(b) All other Local Authorities. By the District Auditor of the Ministry of Health.

The merits or demerits of the different kinds of auditors have been subject to criticism and no one can deny the inconveniences caused by having five different auditors in one municipal borough. However, that is the law as it stands and the auditors' requirements must be anticipated by the book-keeper.

(a) The Elective and Mayor's auditors are easily satisfied where they do not happen to be professional men. They confine themselves generally to checking a few details in the Cash Book and after checking it with the Pass Books it is usually signed as being " audited and found correct."

(b) The professional audit is conducted upon well defined commercial lines and is concerned more particularly with questions of accountancy.

(c) The District Auditor approaches the accounts from a legal standpoint ; he is mainly concerned about the legality of all expenditure incurred.

In all cases the books must be balanced, and all vouchers and other information filed in convenient order for perusal.

(6) The Annual Abstract of Accounts.

The abstract or summary of the accounts of all authorities whose accounts are subject to District Audit as a whole, must be published in the local newspaper (this regulation was suspended during the War).   Under the Municipal Corporations Act, 1882, the abstract of accounts must be published and copies may be obtained by the ratepayers at a reasonable fee.   There is no standard form in which they are prepared but generally the detailed Revenue Accounts and the Balance Sheets of each Fund are given, together with an Aggregate Balance Sheet showing the general financial position of the Corporation.

(7) The Organization of the Account-keeping.

The financial officer of a Local Authority is generally responsible for all the accounts, but it does not always follow that the whole of the book-keeping is done by his staff.   In very large boroughs the detailed book-keeping of the trading undertakings, for instance, may be under the control of a departmental accountant.   The main results only are incorporated in the books of the Borough Treasurer or Accountant.   Again, stores and cost accounts may be kept in the Engineer's Department.   There is no need for such accounts to be duplicated, provided that a good system of staff audit control is in operation, in which case the results can be checked and incorporated in the main system.

(8) The Allocation and Dissection of Accounts.

The best system can be spoilt by a lack of method in allocation.   All invoices should be allocated specifically to their proper accounts in the Ledger by the chief book-keeper immediately they have been passed by the committee concerned.   He must know which fund they are by law chargeable to and the particular estimate under which they are sanctioned.

If the Day Books or Ledgers are in columnar form with dissecting columns he must in addition make an analysis on the invoice for the guidance of the book-keeper in charge of the Expenditure Ledger. The mass of detail required will decide to a great extent the form of the Day Books and Ledgers and is a very large factor when devising a set of books.

CHAPTER III

1. Prescribed Books.
2. Record of Cash Receipts.
3. Record of Cash Payments.
4. Record of Income.
5. Record of Expenditure.
6. Postings.
7. Trading Accounts.

(1) Prescribed Books.

THE Ministry of Health has power under various Acts to issue regulations prescribing the method of book-keeping and accounting for various Local Authorities. This power has only been exercised in a very limited degree and the regulations issued only affect the older class of the authorities subject to its audit.

(1) The Orders dated 14th January, 1867, and 20th March, 1879, prescribe the books to be kept by Overseers, Guardians and parochial officers dealing with the Poor Rate, Lighting and Watching Rate (Act, 1833) and separate rates under the Burial Acts.

(2) The orders dated 22nd March, 1880, relate to the accounts of Local Boards. (Now Urban District Councils.)

(3) The Board of Trade has prescribed the statement of accounts for Electricity Undertakings.

The books mentioned are as follows—

(a) For Urban District Councils—

A MINUTE BOOK which must contain a statement of all moneys paid or received, all orders drawn upon the Treasurer, and any other pecuniary transactions.

A LEDGER in which the items contained in the Minute Book are to be posted under detailed headings. In addition this ledger must contain a personal account with the Treasurer, personal accounts of mortgagees,

17

accounts for expenditure out of loans, etc., and the half-yearly or annual Balance Sheet or Balance Account.

A HIGHWAYS EXPENDITURE ACCOUNT, containing expenditure divided into Manual labour, Team labour, Materials and Miscellaneous.

AN ORDER CHECK BOOK. This book is in triplicate containing the order for materials, the counterfoils and the form of invoice to be rendered.

TREASURER'S ACCOUNT. This is practically the Treasurer's Cash Book which he must balance and sign periodically.

The Surveyor is to keep—

A WAGES ACCOUNT in detail.

A STORES ACCOUNT containing accounts for each article received and issued, with an allocation of expenditure.

A CASH ACCOUNT.

A GENERAL RECEIPT CHECK BOOK for all moneys received by him.

All officers receiving or paying moneys must keep a Cash Account.

The collector of the General District Rate must keep the following books—

THE RATE BOOK.

THE RATE COLLECTION ACCOUNT.

THE COLLECTING AND DEPOSIT BOOK.

THE RECEIPT CHECK BOOK.

(b) For Overseers and Collectors of Poor Rates—

Rate Book.

Book of Receipts and Payments.

Balance Sheet of Receipts and Payments.

General Receipt Book.

Rate Receipt Check Book.

Instalment Rate Receipt Check Book.

Monthly Statements.

Unpaid Rates Statement.

(c) For Collectors of Special Rates—
    Rate Book.
    Rate Receipt and Payment Book.
    Rate Receipt Book.
    Collecting and Deposit Book.
    Monthly Statements.
    Unpaid Rate Statements.

Where, however, the special rate is made on the same day as the Poor Rate within the same area, the Poor Rate Collectors' books may be provided with additional columns for the Special Rate.

It will be seen that the Ministry of Health have not been eager to teach the local authorities book-keeping and the above mentioned regulations were only necessary owing to the slipshod methods of part time officers of the small Urban Districts.

Since the passing of the Municipal Corporations Act, 1882, the larger Local Authorities have appointed financial officers in charge of their accounts, and the development of municipal book-keeping has necessarily been left to those officers.

The books of record used depend upon the size of the Local Authority, but we will assume that the transactions are numerous enough to warrant the employment of a cashier.

(2) Record of Cash Receipts.

The cashier's Cash Book is entered up in detail and analyzed into suitable columns, the totals of which may be entered in the main Cash Book daily or weekly. This procedure applies to all cash handed over to the cashier. Where certain departments pay their receipts direct to the bank a carbon copy of the paying-in slip is sent to the Finance Office and these are entered into the main Cash Book. The same procedure is adopted with the rates collected by independent collectors, but where the collection is centralized, a daily return of payments to bank is furnished by the Chief Rate Clerk which is entered into the Cash Book.

(3) Record of Cash Payments.

All payments are made by cheque and are usually authorized by an order on the treasurer containing a complete list. The cheques when drawn are checked with the authorized list and a copy of the latter is entered into the Cash Book.

Thus far the records from which the Cash Book is written up are fairly simple, there are, however, moneys received direct by the bank which are usually found in the Pass Book if not by direct advice by the bank. Sundry payments, e.g., bank interest, are found in the Pass Book. Apart from these exceptional entries, although it is usual to agree the Cash Book with the Bank Pass Book, there are very serious objections to the practice of writing up the Cash Book from the Pass Book as is often done in small authorities.

(4) Record of Income.

All items of income should be entered in an Income Journal or Day Book. It is important to remember that whereas receipts are mainly entered up from the bank slips, income should be entered up from records of income earned irrespective of and independent of the cash receipt. Some establishment receipts, e.g., Public Conveniences, do in fact agree with the total income journalized, but the debtor in this case is the collector and the income is entered in the Income Journal from his collection book. There should be detailed records the totals of which can be entered into the main Income Journal, the following examples will illustrate the method—

Public Convenience Collection Account.
Town Hall Lettings Register.
Sewer Connections Day Book.
Private Works Day Book.

In the last three the record is entered when the account is rendered and the totals taken weekly or monthly to the Income Journal.

(5) Record of Expenditure.

It is usual when the accounts have been passed by the respective committees concerned to mark each with the particular heading it is chargeable to and then to enter them into an Expenditure Journal in detail.

This book is conveniently ruled to allow for extensions into analysis columns. It will be understood that this is not a copy of the Cash Book monthly payments if it is pointed out that after the close of the year many accounts have not been paid although they are true expenditure in that particular year.

(6) Postings.

All Cash Book entries should be posted in detail to Personal Accounts, which include tradesmen's accounts, collector's accounts, and debtors for work rendered, since cash can only be paid to or received from some person.

The Income Journal entries (including the subsidiary Journals when totals only are carried into the Income Journal) are posted to the debit of their respective personal accounts, and credited in total to the respective heads of Income in the Revenue Ledger. The Expenditure Journal items are credited to their respective personal accounts and debited in total to the respective heads of Expenditure in the Revenue Ledger.

The above outline will give the student an idea of the book-keeping operations and it will be noticed that though many other methods are practised this may claim the merit of being true to the theory of double entry and not inconsistent with modern commercial methods. There is no reason why municipal book-keeping should be singled out for being illogical, fantastical and unscientific.

(7) Trading Accounts.

It is found advisable to keep the accounts of the trading undertakings separate from the Rating Funds ; they may, however, by a sub-division of the books be kept within one cash book and ledger. There is nothing different in the method, however, except that in the place of the Income Journal we have specially ruled books as the Electricity, Gas or Water rental. This book is a personal account in detail and an Income Journal in summary.

As each class of accounts relating to the Rating and non-Rating Funds, the Trading Funds, Capital Expenditure and Loan Funds will be dealt with in detail, exceptional entries will be then explained in their proper relation.

CHAPTER IV

THE RATING FUNDS

1. The Borough Fund.
2. Exchequer Contribution Account.
3. The General District Fund.
4. The County Fund.
5. The General Rate Fund.
6. The expenses of the Smaller Authorities.

(1) The Borough Fund.

THE civic expenses of Municipal Corporations are regulated by the Municipal Corporations Act, 1882, which provides for the creation of a " Borough Fund " to which all the rents and profits of corporate land and other income payable to a municipal corporation shall be carried. The same Fund shall be chargeable with certain payments specified in the 5th schedule to the Act and any other expenditure duly chargeable thereon by Act of Parliament or otherwise by law.

By the provisions of the Local Government Act, 1888, the expenses of a municipal corporation acting as a County Borough are chargeable to the Borough Fund. Various other expenses are also payable out of the Borough Fund, the following being a list of the main heads of expenditure chargeable thereon for municipal and county purposes. It is important to note, however, that in many boroughs the provisions of local Acts may vary the particular fund to which certain expenses are chargeable.

(a) Salaries of Borough Officers (M.C. Act, 1882, Sch. 5).
(b) Office Establishment Charges (M.C. Act, 1882, Sch. 5).
(c) Municipal Buildings (M.C. Act, 1882, Sch. 5.)
(d) Legal and Parliamentary Expenses (M.C. Act, 1882, Sch. 5).
(e) Loan Charges (M.C. Act, 1882, Sch. 5).
(f) Police (M.C. Act, 1882, Sch. 5).
(g) Administration of Justice (M.C. Act, 1882, Sch. 5).
Assizes.
Quarter Sessions.
Petty Sessions.
Coroner's Fees and Expenses (M.C. Act, 1882).
Salary and Expenses of Probation Officer (Probation Officers Act, 1907).
Counsel's Fees (Criminal Appeal Act, 1907).

23

Maintenance of Inebriates (Inebriates Act).
Maintenance of Children in Reformatory and Industrial Schools.
Maintenance of Children under Children's Act, 1908.
(h) Registration of Electors (Representation of the People Act, 1918).
(i) Main Roads and Bridges (Local Government Act, 1888).
(j) Lunatics and Lunatic Asylums (Lunacy Act, 1890).
Loan charges in respect of Buildings, Additions and Alterations and Repairs, Buildings and Repairs Fund.
(k) Public Libraries (Libraries Act, 1919).
(l) Burial Board Deficiency (Burial Acts).
(m) Education Precept (Education Act).
(n) Election Expenses (M.C. Act, 1882).
(o) Small Holdings Deficiency (Small Holdings and Allotments Act).
(p) Tramways Deficiency (Tramways Act, 1870).
(q) Exchequer Contribution Account Deficiency (Local Government Act, 1888).
(r) Estates.
(s) The administration of various Acts as under—
Shop Regulations Acts, 1912.
Weights and Measures Acts.
Contagious Diseases (Animals) Acts.
Sale of Food and Drugs Acts.
Midwives Act, 1902.
Poisons and Pharmacy Act, 1908.
Explosives and Petroleum Acts.
Dogs Act, 1908.
Motor Car Acts.
Locomotive Acts.
Mental Deficiency Act, 1913.

The various items of income relating to the above mentioned purposes, viz., rents and profits of corporate property, fines and penalties under the Act, Justices fines and penalties, Town Hall lettings, licences, etc., are carried to the credit of the fund, together with the proceeds of the Borough Rate.

There are a few special features which require the attention of the book-keeper.

(a) REGISTRATION EXPENSES. The expenses which are part recoverable from the Ministry of Health may be defrayed by the Town Clerk out of advances made to him from the Fund. If done in this way the entry would be to credit Cash and debit the Town Clerk for advances. When the final accounts are made on each register from the information supplied by him, debit Registration and credit Town Clerk. A further entry is necessary to debit

Ministry of Health and credit Registration for proportion repayable. In some boroughs the Finance Officer pays the accounts in the usual way, when of course the account with the Town Clerk does not appear.

(b) SUNDRY ACCOUNTS. Where a proportion of the expenses are repayable by grant from a Government Department, e.g., Mental Deficiency, Places of Detention, etc., ·considerable confusion exists where payments on account are posted direct to Income from the Cash Book; there should be no difficulty where a personal account is kept with the respective Government Departments.

(c) LUNATIC ASYLUMS. The charge falling upon the Borough Fund is the Loan charges and interest in respect of buildings and the annual deficiency of the Repairs Fund which is credited with profits on private patients. Consequently the capital expenditure on Asylums appears in the Borough Fund Balance Sheet instead of that of the Visiting Committee.

(2) Exchequer Contribution Account.

This is a special account which is credited with amounts received from government departments in respect of local taxation licences and estate duties, and customs and excise duties. The customs and excise duties are transferred to the Higher Education Fund in total. The local taxation licences and estate duty grants are to be applied by the provisions of the Local Government Act of 1888 in the following order—

(1) Administration Expenses (Sec. 6 Finance Act, 1908).

(2) Public Vaccinations (L. G. Act, Sec. 24 (2) a).

(3) Boards of Guardians (L. G. Act, Sec. 24 & 26).
Remuneraton of Teachers in Poor Law Schools.
School fees for Pauper Children.
Remuneration of Registrars of Births and Deaths.
Maintenance of Pauper Lunatics.
Costs of Officers of Unions and of District Schools.

(4) Transfer to Borough Fund and other accounts of the corporation for the purpose of salaries of Medical Officers and Sanitary Inspectors. Maintenance of pauper lunatics chargeable to the borough, police pay and clothing.

(5) Other payments under Sec. 23, 1888 Act.

The borough is obliged by Sec. 26 of the 1888 Act to make all payments included in (1), (2) and (3) above, and if the grants are not sufficient then the deficiency must be transferred from the Borough Fund, on the other hand if the grants are more than sufficient to make all the specified payments, the surplus is to be transferred to the Borough Fund or other rate levied over the whole area.

(3) The General District Fund.

The General District Fund was created by the Public Health Act, 1875, and is chargeable with the expenses of authorities acting as sanitary authorities.

The main heads of expenditure are—

Highways Repairs and Upkeep.
Sewers and Sewage Disposal.
Street Improvements.
Scavenging and Dust Collection.
Parks and Pleasure Grounds.
Fire Brigade.
Infectious Diseases Hospitals.
Public Conveniences.
Street Lighting.
Treatment of Tuberculosis.
Maternity and Child Welfare.
Treatment of Venereal Diseases.
Public Baths and Wash-houses.
Public Officers, Salaries and Establishment Expenses.

In the case of urban districts the deficiency on all the trading undertakings would be chargeable thereto, together with the expenses of any of the adoptive Acts.

The Fund is created with the proceeds of the General District Rate which is levied and collected by the Council. It should be noted that many expenses in the administration of special Acts which are chargeable in the case of urban districts to the District Fund are in the case of boroughs chargeable to the Borough Fund.

The general course of book-keeping outlined is applicable to this Fund, but there are one or two special features which are of interest to the book-keeper.

(a) RECORD OF RATE COLLECTION. The rate is a charge levied upon the ratepayers of the district for services to be rendered and is payable in advance. There are many ways of treating this account in the main ledgers, but from a book-keeping standpoint, the entries should record the transactions in their proper sequence. The entries may be as follows—

Dr.	Cr.	
Ratepayers	G.D. Fund Rate A/c	Rate made
Collectors	Ratepayers	Amount collected periodically
Cash	Collectors	Cash banked
G.D. Fund Rate A/c	Ratepayers	Allowances, Empties, etc.

The result of the above entries at the end of the financial year will be that the General District Revenue Account is credited with the net rate collectable, the Ratepayers Account will show a debit balance representing the arrears carried forward and the collectors would be shown as debtors for any amounts collected but not paid to bank.

(b) WAGES. The total weekly amount is debited to a Wages Account and periodically transferred to the proper heads of expenditure. To provide the information for this transfer it is necessary to keep a wages analysis book with suitable columns.

(c) STORES ACCOUNTS. Materials purchased by small Authorities are generally ordered specifically for certain purposes and are charged thereto direct, but in large

Authorities the practice is to take them into store and issue when required. All accounts for materials taken into store are allocated to " Stock Account " and are debited to a Stores Account. Periodically the transfer is made from this account for stores issued to the respective heads of expenditure. This method necessitates a proper system of stores accounts kept by some department of the Corporation. A suitable system will be described in a later chapter.

(4) The County Fund.

The expenses of County Councils, which were created by the Local Government Act, 1888, are payable out of the " County Fund " (Sec. 68), to which also all receipts must be carried. The expenses are classified into " General Expenses," *i.e.*, for purposes which are declared to be general, or purposes for which the County Council may assess the whole area of the county for contributions ; and " Special Expenses," *i.e.*, for any purposes from contributions to which any portion of the county is for the time being exempt.

This expenditure is met by contributions assessed on all the parishes in the county for general expenses and on parishes liable to be assessed for special purposes. The demand is made by the county on the Guardians, who in their turn include it in the precept on the overseers to be collected as part of the Poor Rate.

The main heads of " General " expenditure for a county include expenses in relation to—

County Buildings.
Reformatory and Industrial Schools.
Salaries of Officers, etc.
Main Roads and County Bridges.
Lunatic Asylums.
County Police.
Opposition to Bills.

Administration of Acts *re* Weights and Measures, Rivers Pollution, Diseases of Animals, etc.

Treatment of Tuberculosis.

Maternity and Child Welfare, etc.

" Special " expenditure includes—

Education—Elementary and Higher.

Any purpose for which a portion of the county is exempt or which is chargeable to a limited portion of the county.

LONDON COUNTY COUNCIL. Under the provisions of the 1888 Act the London County Council are invested with additional powers in relation to—

Street Improvements.
Parks.
Fire Brigade.
Sewerage.
Main Drainage.
Housing Acts, etc.

(5) The General Rate Fund.

The Metropolitan Boroughs were created under the London Government Act, 1899. They are subject to control by the London County Council with regard to loan sanctions, etc., and possess less powers than Urban District Councils. The special features of Metropolitan Boroughs include—

(1) A Consolidated Rate called the " General Rate."

(2) The powers and duties of Overseers which are merged in the Council.

(3) They appoint the Assessment Committee.

The General Rate which has all the incidence of a Poor Rate is applied to the following purposes—

Payments to other Authorities—

London County Council.	County Rate Precept.
Guardians of the Poor.	Contribution Order.
Metropolitan Police.	Police Precept.

Metropolitan Water Board.   Precept for Deficiency.
Expenses of Highways.
,,   Public Gardens and Enclosures.
            Sewers.
            Public Lighting.
            Collection of House Refuse.
            Disinfecting.
            Public Offices, Salaries and Establishment
               Expenses.
            Registration of Electors.
            Libraries.
..   Baths and Wash-houses.
,,   Conveniences.

It will be seen that in consequence of the very limited powers of a Metropolitan Borough, the single rate, and the single fund, book-keeping complications are very rare. These facts together with the influence of one government auditor for the whole of the twenty-eight boroughs has had the tendency of producing a system of book-keeping, which in comparison with provincial authorities, may be described as ideal. The principles of double entry are applied with success.

(6) The Expenses of the Smaller Authorities.

(a) RURAL DISTRICT COUNCILS. The expenses are either—
General—Establishment Expenses.
            Disinfection.
            Conveyance of Infected Persons.
            Highways and New Bridges.
            Rights of Way and Commons.
            Licences and all expenses not special.
Special—Sewers.
            Water supply.
            Allotments.
            Housing and all other expenditure stated to be
               special.

(*b*) PARISH COUNCILS. The main items of expenditure
are in respect of—

Holding Meetings.	Allotments and Parks.
Elections.	Pond Nuisances.
Closed Churchyards.	Rights of Way.
Appeals.	Tramways.
Fire Engine.	Postal Facilities.
Public Buildings.	

(*c*) PARISH MEETINGS of parishes where there is no
Parish Council expenses may be incurred in respect of—

Meetings.   Polls.   Tramways and Postal Facilities.

The whole of the above expenses under (*a*), (*b*) and (*c*)
are paid out of the Poor Rate which is levied by the
overseers in respect of these and other expenses.

Sundry other expenses of adoptive Acts may also be
charged to the Poor Rate.

The whole of the expenses of all Authorities up to 1898
is tabulated in the " Appendix to Minutes of Evidence
(Vol. I), Royal Commission on Local Taxation," Part I.
The student is recommended to carefully read the first
eighty pages.

CHAPTER V

IT is difficult to define what a Trading Undertaking of a corporation is, but if we assume that it is one, the profits of which are assessed for income tax, then there would be included waterworks, electricity works, tramways, gasworks, markets, slaughterhouses, ferries, docks, bridges and cemeteries, etc. For the purpose of this chapter we will deal with those which are commonly known as the Trading Undertakings, viz., electricity, tramways, waterworks and gas works.

(1) Electricity Undertaking.

The Statement of Accounts and Balance Sheet must be rendered to the Commissioners of Supply annually in the prescribed form. This form, therefore, will govern the allocation of expenditure and the separation of the items of income. The revenue expenditure is classified as under—

(a) Generation of electricity, including fuel, oilmongery, repairs to buildings and machinery, and salaries and wages at generating station.

(b) Distribution of electricity, salaries of inspectors and outdoor superintendents, wages at transformers station, repairs and maintenance, mains, meters, motors, etc.

(c) Public lamps, attendance and maintenance.

(d) Works executed for customers and goods for sale.

(e) Rents, rates and taxes.

(f) Management and general expenses.

(g) Other charges.

The income is separated under—

(a) Sale of electricity, private lighting, power and heating, bulk supplies, traction supplies, public lighting supplies.

(b) Public lamps. Tending and maintenance.

(c) Works executed for customers and goods sold.

(d) Rentals of meters, motors, etc.

(e) Sundry revenue.

The net Revenue Account would be charged with interest on loans, income tax on profits, loan repayment charges, parliamentary expenses, transfer to reserve fund.

The general principles of book-keeping previously outlined will apply to this undertaking and apart from the special entries relating to capital expenditure and loan charges, which will be dealt with in a separate chapter, the only special feature remaining is the Collection Account, for electricity charges to consumers. For this purpose a special columnar book generally called the Electricity Rental is utilized. This constitutes, like a Rate Book, the Debtors Ledger. This book is prepared from the meter readings which, when priced out, are also used for the preparation of the accounts to be rendered. When complete and totalled it forms the basis of a Journal entry for bringing the income into the Main Ledger, the entries being as under—

Dr.	Cr.
Consumers (Total A/c)	Sales A/c for Electricity Supplied
Collectors	Consumers (Total A/c) for Amount Collected Periodically
Cash	Collectors for Cash Received
Sales A/c	Collectors for Allowances, Empties, etc.

The details of the cash received will, of course, be posted in detail to consumers' credits in the Electricity Rental which is made up quarterly. There are also the accounts which are collected monthly or even weekly. A separate rental is kept for these, and some customers are asked to deposit a certain amount before they can have a supply.

It is absolutely necessary that a proper record of such deposits is kept, and for this purpose a card index will meet the requirements. It should be thoroughly understood, that where in some cases customers are given credit for the amount of deposit at any time, the gross amount of the account should appear in the Rental and not the net amount.

(2) Water Accounts.

There is no prescribed form for these accounts, but the revenue expenses may be conveniently grouped in the following manner—

(a) Collection and storage of water, including pumping, filtration, maintenance and supervision of aqueducts, etc.

(b) Distribution, including salaries of inspectors, repairs and maintenance of mains and meters.

(c) Works executed for customers and goods sold.

(d) Rents, rates and taxes.

(e) Management and general expenses.

(f) Other charges.

The income is divided into water rents and charges, water rate and sundry income. The charges to Net Revenue Account will be similar to those of an Electricity Undertaking. The income is generally derived by charging a percentage on the rateable value of the premises and is frequently collected with the Poor and General District Rates, one Demand Note being used.

This income is incorporated in the Ledger by periodical Journal entries similar to the entries for the rate collection described in Chapter IV. In addition to the charge based on rateable value, water may be charged for in bulk according to the meter records. This necessitates the keeping of a Meter Charges Book which is compiled and the totals journalized in a similar manner to the Electricity Rental.

(3) Tramways Accounts.

There is no form of prescribed accounts but the standard form agreed upon by the Tramways Association and the Institute of Municipal Treasurers is generally adhered to. The revenue expenditure is allocated under the main heads of—

(a) Traffic expenses.

(b) General establishment expenses.

(c) General repairs and maintenance.

(d) Power expenses.

The income is limited, of course, to traffic receipts and sundry items, such as advertising on cars, etc. The peculiar feature of Tramways Accounts is that the income from traffic receipts is on the cash basis. It is a ready money business. In very large undertakings it is usual for the whole of the traffic receipts to be collected, paid into bank and accounted for by the traffic superintendent. He will furnish the Finance Department with a weekly return of traffic receipts and this forms the basis of a Journal entry to bring the income into the Ledger. The entries being—

Dr.	Cr.
Traffic Superintendent	Traffic Receipts A/c for Moneys Received from Conductors
Cash	Traffic Superintendent for Cash Banked

The only possible balance there can be is a debit balance at the end of the financial year on the Traffic Superintendent's Account, for money received by his department which has not been banked.

The net Revenue Account bears the same class of charges as the electricity undertaking.

(4) Gas Works Accounts.

The revenue expenditure of a gas undertaking is classified under the following main heads—

(a) Manufacture of gas, including carbonization, purification, salaries of officers, repairs and maintenance of buildings and plant, oilmongery, etc.

(b) Distribution of gas, salaries and wages, repairs and maintenance of mains, meters and services.

(c) Public lamps, lighting and repairing.

(d) Rents, rates and taxes.

(e) Management and general expenses.

(f) Gas stoves and fittings.

(g) Other expenses.

The income is separated under headings of—

(a) Sale of gas, private consumers, public lamps, meter rents.

(b) Residual products, coke, tar and other products.

(c) Fittings and stoves.

The net Revenue Account is charged with capital charges, etc., previously enumerated.

The accounts relating to the income from the sale of gas are almost identical with those of electricity, but when a gas undertaking develops its residuary products, this necessitates a branch of accounts corresponding with the sales department of an ordinary commercial undertaking.

(5) General Features Applying to Trading Undertakings.

It is safe to say that the accounts of a trading undertaking of a municipality are the nearest approach to that class of accounts which are termed commercial. Compared with the Rating Funds there are one or two distinctive features which usefully may be kept in mind.

(1) The accounts must comprise income and expenditure. There is no question here of merely including cash receipts and cash payments for a financial period.

(2) They are subject to assessment on profits for income tax. This assessment can only be arrived at when the accounts are complete in every respect.

(3) The results of the undertaking are subjected to analysis and criticism in respect of income tax, the charges to customers, and possible charges on the rates

for the deficiency of any year. It is important, therefore, although the accounts themselves do not present many difficulties from the standpoint of book-keeping, that they should be accurate and complete.

(4) Capital expenditure must be clearly set out. The percentage of depreciation on various classes of capital expenditure allowed makes this quite essential.

The whole question of capital expenditure will be dealt with in a separate chapter, but the following is a suggested list of the various heads of expenditure which will be helpful in any case.

(a) APPLYING TO THE FOUR UNDERTAKINGS—
  Acquisition of undertaking where acquired from a
    company.
  Land.
  Buildings.
  Machinery.
  Plant and tools.
  Parliamentary expenses.
  Office furniture.

(b) APPLYING TO WATER WORKS, ELECTRICITY AND
GAS—
  Mains.
  Meters.
  Services.

(c) APPLYING TO WATER WORKS ONLY—
  Aqueducts.
  Compensation works.
  Filter beds.
  Wells.
  Pumping stations.

(d) APPLYING TO GAS WORKS ONLY—
  Lamp posts and lamps.

(e) APPLYING TO ELECTRICITY ONLY—
  Accumulators.
  Instruments.

(*f*) APPLYING TO TRAMWAYS ONLY—
Electrical equipment of line.
Permanent way.
Cars.
Other rolling stock.
Miscellaneous equipment.

(6) The Acquisition of an Undertaking by a Corporation.

It is questionable if it is the correct method to debit the whole cost of the acquisition to a Ledger Account under that heading. Many difficulties arise afterwards owing to the lack of information in this respect. If, for instance, a corporation paid £100,000 for a gas undertaking, lock, stock and barrel, there should, at the time of purchase, be an allocation under the respective capital heads of expenditure above mentioned, showing how the £100,000 is arrived at in the cost. It frequently happens, where a business is bought up, that the purchaser takes over certain trade liabilities ; if so, this should be clearly set out in the books of the corporation. On the acquisition of the undertaking the Journal entries in the corporation's books would be—

(*a*) Debit accounts for the various assets acquired and the goodwill, if any, and credit the vendor company and any liabilities that may be taken over. The goodwill, which of course in a trading undertaking with statutory powers is considerable, will be the difference between the actual assets acquired less the liabilities and the purchase consideration payable to the vendor company.

(*b*) Debit the vendor company and credit Capital Account Cash, etc., representing the discharge of the purchase consideration.

CHAPTER VI

(1) Definition of Capital.

THE word " capital " is commonly used by economists, merchants and accountants, and has a variety of meanings. Much confusion arises out of its indiscriminate use, and for the benefit of the reader the following descriptions of its meaning are given—

(*a*) IN ECONOMICS. *Capital* is that part of a person's possessions which he constitutes as his fund for the purpose of reproduction. It is divided into fixed and circulating, and also positive and negative.

Fixed capital is wealth expended upon land, buildings, etc., retained to produce additional wealth.

Circulating capital is wealth used in the production of commodities, the character of which is changed by a single use, as raw material and cash for the payment of wages.

Positive capital relates to material objects, as land, buildings, stock in trade, etc.

Negative capital is composed of credit, such as the right to demand payment of a debt.

(*b*) IN ACCOUNTANCY. *The capital of a company* relates to its share capital, which is sub-divided into authorized capital, issued capital, unissued capital, paid up capital and uncalled capital.

The capital of a partnership is the amount which stands to the credit of the Partners' Capital Accounts.

The capital of a sole trader is the amount standing to the credit of his personal account, which should equal the excess of the assets over the liabilities.

The capital of an estate in executorship accounts is the total value of a man's possessions at the date of his death after proper apportionment has been made at that date.

(c) IN COMMERCIAL PARLANCE. There are various expressions used which have now come to have a definite meaning attached to them. *The capital employed in a business* is taken to be all the wealth put into it to start and keep it going.

Working capital is generally meant to be that amount of floating assets, viz., cash and stock necessary to run the business.

Capital is often used in the sense that it is the fund from which interest is derived.

(2) Capital Expenditure.

In the commercial sense this means the expenditure necessary to place a company or firm in a position to earn revenue. In the case of a company this capital expenditure is not only met out of money provided by shareholders but that raised by mortgage debentures or other forms of loan sometimes referred to as loan capital.

(3) Municipal Capital Expenditure.

The term " capital expenditure " as applied to Municipal Authorities has its root idea in the economic and commercial theories but is necessarily restricted by legislation. It may be taken to mean all expenditure for which a sanction to borrow may be obtained, the loan being repayable over a period of years. Where money has actually been borrowed it is described as expenditure out of loans. As the principles which have governed the decisions of the Government to sanction the borrowing of money are not inconsistent with commercial ideas it is somewhat futile to describe the expenditure out of such loans as " deferred revenue expenditure."

(4) The Double Account System.

Local Authorities must clearly distinguish in their accounts between expenditure out of loans and other expenditure and this is generally effected by adopting what is known as the Double Account system or a modification of it. The object of this system is to show what capital has been raised and what capital has been expended. To do this the Balance Sheet is in effect divided into two parts, the first being called the Capital Account and showing upon the credit side the capital receipts to date, and upon the debit side the expenditure to date, the balance or the totals of each side being carried to the Balance Sheet proper, which contains in addition the Revenue Balance Sheet items.

(5) The Treatment of Capital Expenditure in the Books of a Local Authority.

In order to produce the information required it is desirable to keep in connection with each undertaking or rate fund a separate Capital Cash Account, which is debited with all moneys borrowed and credited with all payments on account of purposes for which sanctions have been obtained. It is necessary to keep a Capital Ledger, the accounts of which are separated according to the specific sanctions. The totals of these accounts are summarized and carried to the capital portion of the Balance Sheet.

Thus far no particular difficulty presents itself from the book-keeper's standpoint, but the transactions which arise by the extinction of debt are so varied that it may be useful to have the entries set out in detail. It must be remembered that the sanction of the Government department always stipulates that the money borrowed must be repaid within a certain period. The method of repayment depends upon either the arrangement made with the lender or the particular manner in which the money is borrowed, for instance by a stock issue.

(6) The Repayment of Loans.

(a) Repayment of moneys borrowed on mortgage by equal annual instalments.

Dr.	Cr.
Capital Cash A/c	Mortgagee for money borrowed
Mortgagee	Revenue Cash (annual instalment and interest repaid)
Loan Charges Revenue A/c	Mortgagee for Interest
Do. do.	Redemption of Debt A/c (instalment of loan repaid)

(b) Repayment of money borrowed on mortgage by equal annual sums of principal and interest combined (annuity).

The entries are similar to those in (a), but it is necessary to split the annual sum into its proper proportion of principal and interest. A schedule giving this information is invariably attached to the mortgage deed itself. It should be noted that money borrowed must be repaid within the period given in the sanction and it is usual where money is borrowed on mortgage security repayable by instalments that the period for repayment is arranged as near as can be to coincide with the term of the sanction.

(c) Repayment by Sinking Fund method.

This method is adopted where the loans raised by the issue of stock are repayable at a fixed future date. The sinking fund is created for each sanction to which the money is applied. The Rate Fund or trading undertaking is charged with annual contributions which if invested will accumulate at the end of the sanction period a sufficient sum to repay the debt. It will be seen that if separate sinking funds (which may run into hundreds) are set up in the main books many difficulties would arise, but this is met by the operation of a Consolidated

Loans Fund which is practically a " pool " of all the sinking funds relating to the redemption of debt created by an issue of stock.

The operations of the Consolidated Loans Fund are described in the next chapter, so that it is only necessary here to enumerate the entries in the books of the Rating Fund or trading undertaking to which stock has been allocated.

The entries may be as follows—

Dr.	*Cr.*
Capital Cash	Sundry Stockholders : for Stock allocated
Loans Charges Revenue A/c	Consolidated Loans Fund : for Interest on Stock
Do. do.	Consolidated Loans Fund : for Sinking Fund contributions
Consolidated Loans Fund	Revenue Cash : for Interest and Sinking Fund contributions
Investments and Cash (C.L.F.)	Sinking Funds : for annual Sinking Fund contributions
Do. do.	Sinking funds : for annual accumulations

(7) Mortgage Loans Fund.

Where capital money is raised by Short Term Mortgages it is desirable to create a pooling fund in order to keep the operations clear.

The operations on the Fund are comprised in the following Journal entries—

Dr	*Cr*
Loans Fund (Cash)	Mortgagees : Loans received
Loans advanced Account	General District Fund, etc : Advances to various Funds.
General District Fund, etc.	Loans Fund Cash : Payment of advances.
Do. do.	" Advances Repaid Account " : Instalments due.
General District Fund, etc.	Contributions for Interest Account (net) due from Funds.
Cash	General District Fund, etc. : Interest paid to Fund.
Sundry Mortgagees	Cash : Loans repaid to Mortgagees.
Do. do. (Interest A/c)	Cash : Net interest paid to Mortgagees.

The credit balance on the Loans Fund will represent the fund available for either repayment of loans or further appropriations for capital purposes.

The Balance Sheet will show on the asset side the various funds as debtors to the Loans Fund for loans appropriated, and the cash balance. On the liability side sundry mortgages for (1) loans appropriated and (2) loans unappropriated represented by the balance on the Loans Fund.

(8) Capital Expenditure not out of Loans.

It frequently happens that where a local authority could obtain sanction to borrow for a certain purpose the council decides to charge the cost direct to revenue. If this is not capitalized it is lost as a record of expenditure for future reference. There are also certain properties which may be given to the corporation requiring similar treatment.

The entries in the books will be made at the close of the financial year.

Dr.	*Cr.*
(1) Capital Outlay	Permanent Works paid for out of Revenue
(2) Capital Outlay	Property acquired by Gift

The credits will appear on the Balance Sheet grouped under the heading " Excess of Assets over Liabilities " or " Provision made towards Capital Outlay " with Loan Redemption Account Sinking Funds in hand, etc.

CHAPTER VII

(1) Stock Regulations.

THE provisions regulating the issue and the redemption of stock are contained either in a local Act under which the Authority has issued stock, or in the stock regulations of the Ministry of Health. Where stock is issued under the powers of the local Act, the fund which is operated upon is generally named the Consolidated Loans Fund. Under the stock regulations two funds are named, the Dividends Fund and the Redemption Fund. These two latter accounts are merely divisions of the Consolidated Loans Fund. I will, for purposes of describing the entries, adhere to the title of Consolidated Loans Fund as from the book-keeping standpoint no differences are involved.

(2) Description of Stock.

The issue of stock is a method of borrowing money through the medium of the money market for the purposes of various sanctions. The money raised is amalgamated and carried to the credit of a stock fund which can be applied for the purposes of the sanction, the lenders who contribute to the stock or fund being called stock-holders. The operations on the Consolidated Loans Fund will relate therefore to the issue of stock, its management and its redemption.

(3) Issue of Stock.

We will assume that a corporation raises a stock of £1,000,000 at 95 per cent., the financial officer of the corporation acting as registrar. The brokerage of 2s. 6d.

per cent. is paid and the other costs of issue amount in total to £1,500; the Journal entries in connection with the Consolidated Loans Fund will be as follows—

	Dr.	Cr.
	£	£
Application and Allotment A/c . .	950,000	
Discount A/c	50,000	
To Sundry Stockholders . . .		1,000,000
For stock allotted.		
Stock Allocation A/c	1,000,000	
To General District Fund . . .		500,000
Borough Fund		500,000
Being allocation of the Stock to the Sundry Funds according to the sanctions.		
NOTE.—Although the stock is issued at a discount the full nominal value of the Stock is allocated to the specific funds, it being the full amount of their liability for redemption.		
Costs of Issue	1,500	
To Sundry Persons . . .		1,500
Being costs of Brokerage, £1,250 ; Printing, etc., £250.		
General District Fund	25,750	
Borough Fund	25,750	
To Discount A/c		50,000
„ Costs of Issue		1,500
Being discount and costs of issue chargeable to the borrowing funds.		

NOTE.—The funds will have sanctions covering costs of issue which are treated as capital expenditure.

The cash book entries in relation to the above are as under—

CONSOLIDATED LOANS CASH BOOK.

Dr.	£	Cr.	£
To Stockholders .	950,000	By Sundry Persons—	
		Printing . .	250
		Brokerage . .	1,250
		„ Gen. District Fund.	474,250
		„ Borough Fund .	474,250
	950,000		950,000

It will be seen that the effect of the issue of £1,000,000 stock is to produce £948,500 net, which is transferred to the borrowing funds to create a liability of £1,000,000 which has to be provided for by these same funds.

The entries in the books of the General District Fund will be—

	Dr.	Cr.
	£	£
Capital Cash A/c	474,250	
Costs of Issue	25,750	
To Consolidated Loans Fund. . .		500,000

(4) Management of Stock.

The Consolidated Loans Fund will receive from each borrowing fund its proper proportion of dividends payable to stock-holders and in turn pay out the same to the stock-holders. The entries in connection with this are, of course, simple, but I suggest it will save complications if the interest is received from the funds net, *i.e.*, after deducting income tax. This will be found to facilitate the working of the Income Tax Accounts on the Rating Funds.

(5) Redemption of Stock.

The Consolidated Loans Fund must build up a sum sufficient to redeem the stock at par or otherwise, as regulated at the date stipulated for its redemption. A separate Redemption Fund is kept for each issue of stock. The Sinking Fund contributions are received from each borrowing fund and are either invested or utilized for the extinction of stock by purchase on the market.

We will assume that the sum of £25,000 is received from the General District Fund and Borough Fund in equal proportions for Sinking Fund contributions, that of this £20,000 is invested by lending to another Local Authority at 6 per cent. interest, and that £4,000 is utilized in purchasing stock for cancellation. The entries on the Consolidated Fund will be as follows—

	Dr.	Cr.
	£ 25,000	£
General District Fund, etc. . .. . To Consolidated Loans Fund (Redemption A/c) . . . . . . For one year's Sinking Fund contributions.		25,000
Cash. To Gen. District Fund, etc., to close above entry.		
Borrowing Corporation Investment A/c . To Cash . . . . . . For sum lent on Mortgage.	20,000	20,000
Redemption A/c . . . . . To Brokers . . . . . For £5,000 Stock purchased at 80, including Brokerage.	4,010	4,010
Stock-holders A/c . . . . . To Stock Allocation . . . . For Stock redeemed.	5,000	5,000

The effect of this entry is to charge the Redemption Account with the redemption and to reduce the liability of the Contributing Fund to the extent of stock extinguished.

(6) A Consolidated Loans Fund Balance Sheet.

This can now be drawn showing the effect of the foregoing entries—

CONSOLIDATED LOANS FUND BALANCE SHEET.

Dr.			Cr.	£
Corporation 6% Stock :			Allocation of Loans—	
Issued.	Cancelled.	Balance.	General District Fund	497,500
£1,000,000	£5,000	£995,000	Borough Fund .	497,500
				995,000
Redemption Fund			Redemption Fund—	
Accumulations .		20,990	Investments . .	20,000
			Cash in hand . .	990
		1,015,990		1,015,990

(7) Transferred Stock.

Where Sinking Fund accumulations are utilized for new capital purposes instead of being invested it is provided in the stock regulations that where such an amount is withdrawn from the Redemption Fund and applied to a fresh sanction, an equal amount of stock shall be treated as if redeemed by the fund to which it belongs and the liability transferred to the fund in respect of which the statutory borrowing power is exercised.

Assume that the sum of £5,000 is taken from the Redemption Fund accumulated by the General District Fund and applied to the purposes of sanctions in the Electricity Fund the entries in the Consolidated Loans Fund would be as under—

	Dr.	Cr.
	£	£
Redemption A/c	5,000	
To Electricity Fund		5,000
For amount to be applied to new capital purposes.		
Electricity Fund	5,000	
To Cash		5,000
To close above entry.		

There will be two other entries necessary for the purpose of treating the stock as if it were redeemed by the General District and created in respect of the Electricity Fund—

	Dr.	Cr.
	£	£
Stockholders (1st Issue) . . .	5,000	
To Gen. District Fund Allocation A/c .		5,000
For Stock treated as redeemed.		
Electricity Fund Allocation A/c . .	5,000	
To Stockholders (Transferred Stock) .		5,000
For Stock liability transferred to Electricity Fund.		

4—(1763)

Assume that the £5,000 is applied to new sanctions in the same fund, General District Fund; then the entries would be—

	Dr.	Cr.
Redemption A/c . . . . . To General District Fund . . . For amount to be applied to new sanctions.	5,000	5,000
General District Fund . . . . To Cash . . . . . . To close above entry.	5,000	5,000
Stockholders (1st Issue) . . . To Gen. District Fund (Allocation A/c)	5,000	5,000
For Stock to be treated as if redeemed— General District Fund Allocation A/c . To Stock holders (Transferred Stock) . For Transferred Stock liability transferred.	5,000	5,000

It will be seen that three things have happened in the Consolidated Loans Fund, viz.—

(1) The accumulation of the Redemption Fund.

(2) The extinction of debt by the purchase of stock.

(3) The application of accumulations by the method of transferring stock.

All these facts must be recorded in the books of the contributing funds to which they relate by the following suggested entries—

(1) ACCUMULATIONS. The contributing fund will have credited its Sinking Fund with the annual contributions and debited the Consolidated Loans Fund (Cash Investment Account), to give effect to the benefit derived from

the investments of such funds ; it is necessary at the end of the financial year to make a supplementary entry—

Consolidated Loans Fund Cash Investments To Sinking Fund . . . . For net accumulations during the year.		

(2) REDEMPTION OF DEBT BY PURCHASE. The entry will be—

	Dr.	Cr.

Consolidated Loans Fund Stock allocation.
  To Redemption of Debt   .   .   .
For Stock redeemed by purchase   .   .
Sinking Fund   .   .   .   .   .
  To Consolidated Loans Fund Investments
    and Cash   .   .   .   .   .
For Stock redeemed out of accumulations.		

(3) (a) TRANSFERRED STOCK—

To another contributing fund   .   .
Consolidated Loans Fund Stock allocation .
  To Redemption of Debt   .   .   .
For Stock extinguished by transfer .   .
Sinking Fund   .   .   .   .   .
  To Consolidated Loans Investments and
    Cash   .   .   .   .   .   .
For accumulation applied to other capital
  purposes in another contributing fund.		

(b) STOCK TRANSFERRED WITHIN THE FUND—

Consolidated Loans Fund Stock allocated .
  To Redemption of Debt   .   .   .
For Stock extinguished by transfer .   .
Sinking Fund   .   .   .   .   .
  To Consolidated Loans Fund (Invest-
    ments and Cash)   .   .   .   .
For accumulations applied to other Capital
  purposes   .   .   .   .   .   .
Capital Cash .   .   .   .   .   .
  To Consolidated Loans Fund (Trans-
    ferred Stock)   .   .   .   .
For cash received in respect of new Capital
  purposes by which the Stock liability is
  attached to transferred stock.		

(8) Sundry Credits to the Redemption Account of the Consolidated Loans Fund.

There are sundry items which may be taken to the credit of the fund to be utilized for the general purposes thereof—

(*a*) RENTS AND PROFITS OF ANY LAND.   This applies to property and land acquired for any purpose in respect of which statutory borrowing power is exercised by the issue of stock.   Before doing so a deduction may be made for any costs and expenses incurred in respect of the collection of such rents.   This involves keeping two accounts, viz., Rent Account, which is credited with rents received, and an Expenses Account, which may be called rates, taxes, insurances, etc.

The expenses are transferred at the close of the year to the debit of the Rent Account, the balance of which is carried to the Dividends Account of the Consolidated Loans Fund.

(*b*) UNEXPENDED CAPITAL CASH BALANCES.   Assume that the General District Fund has balances totalling to £385 to transfer, the entries will be as follows—

	Dr.	Cr.
	£	£
CONSOLIDATED LOANS FUND. General District Fund . . . . To Redemption A/c . . . . For Cash Balance to be transferred.	385	385
Cash . . . . To General District Fund . . . Cash to close above entry.	385	385
GENERAL DISTRICT FUND. C.L. Fund (Investments and Cash) . . To Capital Cash A/c . . . . Being Transfer of Cash balances to the Consolidated Loans Fund.	385	385

(*c*) SALE OF LAND OR PROPERTY.   Assume that a portion of Corporation land (Borough Fund) was sold for £400 and the proceeds are transferred to the Redemption Fund, the entries would be as follows—

	Dr.	Cr.
BOROUGH FUND. Capital Cash . . . . . . To Capital Expenditure A/c . . . For sale of land. This reduces the Expenditure Account on the Balance Sheet.	£ 400	£ 400
C.L. Fund Investments and Cash . . To Capital Cash A/c . . . For Transfer of Cash balance.	400	 400
CONSOLIDATED LOANS FUND. Borough Fund . . . . . To Redemption A/c . . . . For proceeds of sale of land.	400	 400
Cash . . . . To Borough Fund . . . . Cash to close above entry.	400	 400

NOTE.—The effect of (a), (b) and (c) will be to increase the accumulations in the Redemption Account, benefit for which is given to the contributing funds at the end of the financial year.

(9) Sinking Funds.

All authorities who have created stock are required to furnish annually to the Ministry of Health an abstract of the Stock and Redemption Fund accounts in the form prescribed. This form is practically a summary of the Sinking Funds relating to the stock issues.

A Sinking Fund must be kept in respect of each sanction (of which there may be hundreds), the grand total of which will agree with the amount standing to the credit of the redemption accounts of each issue.

The Sinking Fund may be either—

(a) NON-ACCUMULATING, i.e., by payment to the f nd throughout the prescribed period of such equal sum₁₁as will together amount to the moneys for the repayment of which the Sinking Fund is formed or

(*b*) ACCUMULATING, *i.e.*, by payment to the fund throughout the prescribed period of such equal annual sums as with accumulations at a rate not exceeding (x) pounds per cent. per annum will be sufficient to pay off within the prescribed period the moneys for the repayment of which the Sinking Fund is formed.

It should be borne in mind that the prescribed period is that of the specific sanction and not the period in which the stock must be redeemed. The fund to redeem the stock will be sufficient provided the sanctions of the capital purposes fall within the period of the stock redemption, otherwise at the time the stock is due to be repaid recourse would have to be made to fresh borrowings.

CHAPTER VIII

MISCELLANEOUS FUNDS

(1) Housing Accounts (General.)

A LOCAL Authority may provide houses for the working classes and for that purpose raise loans. Although the expenses are chargeable to the General District Fund, like any other Public Health administration, it is usual to keep separate accounts. The Housing Fund will contain the usual accounts in respect of capital outlay, and a Revenue Account which is debited with all expenditure in respect of loan charges and maintenance, and credited with all income from rents, etc. The surplus or deficiency on the account should be transferred annually to the General District Fund.

It is sometimes the practice to treat " Housing " as part of the General District Fund, which may have the effect of hiding the results, whereas the separate accounts bring out the question of the sufficiency of the rents charged from time to time.

ASSISTED HOUSING SCHEMES. Under the provisions of the Housing and Town Planning Act, 1919, it is the duty of Local Authorities to prepare housing schemes and to carry them out when approved by the Ministry of Health.

It is provided by regulations that separate accounts shall be kept, the object being to ascertain the apportionment of deficiency as between the Treasury and the Local Authority.

Certain restrictions have been placed upon expenditure chargeable to the account, and detailed instructions have been issued as to the manner of keeping the accounts which are also subject to audit by the District Auditor.

(a) *The scope of the accounts.* Full and detailed accounts must be kept in order to provide the details for the annual preparation of a Revenue Account and Balance Sheet.

The Revenue Account must give the following heads of expenditure—

> Loan charges.
> Rents (if any).
> Rates (if paid by Local Authority).
> Taxes.
> Insurances. ˙
> Water charges (if paid by Local Authority).
> Repairs and maintenance.
> Supervision and collection of rents.
> Other expenditure (if any).

On the Income side—

> Rents (including rates and water charges where these are paid by the Local Authority).
> *Less* allowance for uncollected rents and unoccupied houses.
> Other sources of income.
> Produce of 1d. rate for the year.

The Balance Sheet as prescribed is as under—

HOUSING (ASSISTED SCHEME)—BALANCE SHEET.

Capital Liabilities.	Capital Assets.
Stock or Loans outstanding	Houses and other property*
Prospective purchasers' advances	Loans owing to the Council
Overspent Loan balances	Sinking Funds (Investments and Cash)
	Loan moneys in hand
	Sundry Debtors

* The asset to be shown at original cost. Only those properties which remain in the possession of the authority are to be included on the Balance Sheet. Either on the Balance Sheet or in connection therewith, the balances connected with each authorized borrowing are to be separately entered in such manner as to show their due correspondence.

Capital Outlay Discharged.
By Loan Repayment
By Sinking Fund provisions
By direct charge on revenue

Deferred Charges.
Expenses of Stock or Bond issues
Discounts on Stock issues

Revenue Liabilities.
Tradesmen and Others
Income Tax unpaid
Unclaimed Dividends
Other special liabilities
Overspent Cash balances

Revenue Assets.
Rents uncollected
Exchequer subsidy receivable
Rate contribution receivable
Other uncollected income
Repairs Fund investments
Cash balances in hand
Materials in hand

Fund Balances.
Repairs Fund
Revenue Account

Fund Deficiencies.
Revenue Account

It will be seen that in this case a mere abstract of receipts and payments, the only system of accounts known to most of the small authorities will not be sufficient, and that the principles of double entry book-keeping is insisted upon.

(b) *The legal limits upon expenditure chargeable.* As the expected annual deficiency on the account is borne by the Local Authority to the extent of a penny rate and the balance by the Treasury, certain restrictions are operative.

(1) LOAN CHARGES. No actual rate of interest is fixed which a local authority can pay; it must, however, not vary very much from the interest in force for loans advanced by the Public Works Loan Commissioners. The interest should be approved by the Ministry of Health.

(2) REPAIRS AND MAINTENANCE. This is fixed at 15 per cent. of the gross estimated rent.

(3) SUPERVISION AND MANAGEMENT. The limit is fixed at 5 per cent. of the gross estimated rent.

(4) RENT CHARGEABLE TO TENANTS. The rent is fixed as the amount necessary to cover interest on two-thirds of the capital cost of land, development and buildings, plus allowance for unoccupied houses, repairs and maintenance, supervision and collection of rents, insurance

and depreciation. The rent will be reconsidered after 31st March, 1927.

(5) NET RENT. This is the gross rent less 5 per cent. in respect of uncollected rents and empties.

(6) PRODUCE OF A PENNY RATE. The rate shall be taken to be the amount actually realized during the financial year as certified by the District Auditor.

The local authority in respect of (2) repairs and (3) supervision is limited to fixed percentages and such percentage in respect of repairs should be taken to the credit of a fund.

(c) *The books to be kept.* Housing Order No. 487 prescribes in detail the accounts to be kept, as under—

IMPERSONAL ACCOUNTS.

For Expenditure—Loan Repayments
                            Loan Interest
                            Rates, Rents, Insurances, etc.
                            Management Expenses
                            Repairs, etc.

For Income—Rent Income Account
                    Rate Contribution Account
                    Exchequer Subsidy Account

The balances of the foregoing accounts will be transferred to a Fund Account called the Housing (Assisted Scheme) Revenue Account.

PERSONAL ACCOUNTS.

Officers { Treasurer's Cash Book
Rent Collectors
Storekeepers' Accounts

Debtors { Tenants (Rent Account)
Council (Rate Contribution Account)
Ministry (Exchequer Subsidy Account)
Mortgagors' Accounts
Investments Accounts

Creditors { Mortgagees' Accounts
Inland Revenue (Income Tax) Account
Other Creditors, *e.g.*, Tradesmen
Tenants' (Deposits) Account
Purchasers' (Instalments) Account

In connection with capital outlay this must be separated into—

Capital Asset Accounts.

Deferred Charges Accounts.

Discharged Capital Outlay Account.

Where loans are repaid by contributions to Sinking or Redemption Funds the following accounts must be kept—

Sinking Fund Contributions Account (Revenue Expenditure).

Sinking or Redemption Fund (Fund Account).

Sinking Fund Investment Account.

Sinking Fund Expenses Account.

The student who has followed my outline of the principles of double entry in Chapter I will realize that what may have seemed theoretical has actually been adopted in the requirements of assisted housing schemes. Let us assume that a small District Council has executed an approved scheme for fifty houses and that they have been let for a year. The book-keeping entries would be as follows—

Dr.			Cr.	
1. Cash . .	£50,000	Public Works Commissioners	For Loan advanced	
2. Capital Assets	50,000	Builders . £40,000 Landowner 10,000	Buildings, Streets, etc. Land	
3. Builder .	40,000	Cash } . 50,000	To close above entries	
4. Landowner.	10,000	„ }		

(The above is in respect of Capital outlay.)

5. Tenants .	£2,500	Rent Income A/c	For Rents due	
6. Rent Collector	2,400	Tenants	For Rents collected	
7. Cash .	2,400	Collector	For Cash paid to Bank	
8. Rent Income	50	Tenants	For Empties, etc.	
9. Management Expenses .	|125	Council	Proportion of Expenses	
10. Rates, Rents, Insurances	50	Creditors Tradesmen	Expenses incurred	
11. Council .	125	} Cash	To Close 9 and 10	
12. Creditors .	50			
13. Repairs A/c	375	Repairs Fund	Amount allowed	
14. Repairs Fund	75	Tradesmen	Actual Repairs	
15. Tradesmen .	75	Cash	To close 14	
16. Council .	100	Rate Contribution Account	1d. rate subsidy	
17. Loan Repayment .	500	Discharged Capital Account	Loan repaid	
18. Interest .	3,000	Public Works Commissioners	Interest on Loan	
19. Public Works Commissioners . .	3,500	Cash	To close 18 and part 1	

The Revenue Account would be made up—

	£			£
To Managem't Expenses	125	By Rents . . .		2,500
„ Rates, Taxes, etc. .	50	Less Losses . .		50
„ Repairs . . .	375			—
„ [Loan Repayment .	500			2,450
„ Interest . . .	3,000	„ Rate Subsidy .		100
		„ Exchequer Subsidy		1,500
	£4,050			£4,050

REPAIRS FUND.

	£		£
To Repairs . . .	75	By amount charged to	
„ Balance to Balance		Revenue Account	375
Sheet . . .	300		
	£375		£375

The Balance Sheet will be as under—

Capital Liabilities.	£	*Capital Assets.*	£
Loans Outstanding .	49,500	Houses . . .	50,000
Capital outlay discharged by Loan repayment .	500		
	£50,000		£50,000

Revenue Liabilities.		*Revenue Assets.*		
Overspent Cash Balance	1,350	Rents uncollected	50	
		Exchequer Subsidy receivable	1,500	
		Rate contributions receivable .	100	
				1,650

Fund Balances.		*Fund Deficiencies*	—
Repairs Fund . .	300	.	
	£51,650		£51,650

The above *pro forma* accounts are limited to the most elementary transactions : there may be special features which call for specific treatment.

(a) *Repairs Fund investments.* It will be seen that there is £300 to the credit of this account which should, if possible, be invested.

(b) *Loan charges.* The procedure will be the same as outlined in a previous chapter on Loan Accounts.

(c) *Purchase of houses.* When a house is sold it may be at a price which is less than the actual cost. Assume that a house which cost £1,000 is sold for £800 the entries will be as follows—

	Dr.	Cr.
	£	£
Purchasers' Account	800	
Discharged Capital Outlay Account . .	200	
To Capital Asset		1,000

This entry has the effect of taking the cost of the asset out of the Capital Asset Account and taking the loss of £200 to that section of the Balance Sheet under the heading of Deferred Charges. The money received shall be carried to the account called the Proceeds of Sale (Cash) Account, which, subject to the direction of the Ministry, shall be charged with Sinking Fund contributions and the balance invested.

(d) *Capital outlay.* The expenditure out of loans is divided into two classes, viz. : (1) *Capital assets,* to which is taken the actual cost of lands, roads, sewers and houses ; and (2) Deferred charges, which are represented by expenses and discounts in connection with the flotation of loans and the loss on sale of houses. These two classes are to be treated differently in the books : the former will stand at the original cost, and the latter will be written down each year by the amount of loan repayments applicable thereto.

(2) Private Streets.

Where the Local Authority decides to make up any street (not being a highway repairable by the inhabitants at large) it may apportion the cost of the work on the respective owners of property fronting, adjoining or abutting on the same. The work entailed is as follows—

(*a*) The preparation of an estimate of the probable cost. The frontagers have a right to inspect the detailed accounts and to lodge any objection.

(*b*) Cost Accounts of the work executed where done by the Corporation.

(*c*) The apportionment of the cost amongst the persons chargeable.

(*d*) The collection of amounts charged.

The book-keeping is varied according to the method of procedure, *e.g.*, if the provisions of the Public Health Act are applied, the work is done first and the charges collected afterwards. Under some Acts the apportionment of estimated cost may be collected before the work is done. Another variation is where the work is done by a contractor instead of being done by direct labour.

The book-keeping entries will be as follows—

(*a*) Debit " Street " Account with the cost of the work. If the work is done by a contractor the corresponding credit will be to the contractor's personal account. If done by the corporation, the wages, materials, etc., will be charged direct to the account, or if there is a proper costing system the expenditure is transferred in total from the fund to which the Works Department is attached.

(*b*) Debit the frontagers' personal accounts with the apportionments and credit the " Street " account.

(*c*) Where the estimated apportionment is collectible before the work is done, the transaction is simply a cash one, the frontagers being credited with the cash on account of work to be done.

A register should be kept of estimated and actual apportionments, and this may in some cases be adapted for the owners' personal accounts in a tabular form.

The local authority may, where it is considered desirable, borrow money for the purpose of carrying out the work and the interest thereon is as far as practicable to be recovered from the frontagers.

The question of interest arises where owners are allowed to pay by instalments, the General District Fund (which in the first instance is chargeable with the interest on the loan) being credited with the interest on amounts outstanding and the owners debited.

(3) Mental Hospital Accounts.

County Councils and County Boroughs must provide asylums for the accommodation of pauper and private patients. The general management of the hospital is vested in the Visiting Committee, which must be appointed annually by the local authority providing the hospital. The accounts for county asylums are subject to the District Audit and the Financial Statement has the following divisions—

(1) Maintenance Account.
(2) Buildings and Repairs Account.
(3) Farming and Gardening Account.

There are one or two features which are peculiar to Mental Hospital Accounts, viz.—

(a) The Maintenance Account is designed so as to furnish the information as to the weekly cost per head. At the commencement of the year an estimate is prepared and the cost per head is fixed, this being the charge made to the guardians for pauper patients.

(b) Where private patients are taken the minimum charge is generally based on the cost for pauper patients plus an amount representing the capital charges on the institution. The full rate is credited to the Maintenance Account and a transfer made by debiting Maintenance Account and crediting Building and Repair Account with the amount charged in excess of the pauper rate.

(c) Buildings and Repairs Fund. This fund is debited with the annual cost of repairs, small additions and improvements. It is credited with the surplus charge for private patients referred to in paragraph (b) and the balance is recoverable by precept on the County Council or County Borough.

(d) The Farm and Garden Account is practically a Profit and Loss Account of the farm. It is debited with labour, provender, seeds and manures, and purchases of live and dead stock. The produce is charged to the hospital at its market price and the stock being brought into account the result is transferred to Maintenance Account.

(e) Superannuation. All employees belong to the Superannuation Fund, paying contributions at a rate varying with the length of service. The contributions are carried to the credit of Maintenance Account, and pensions when they become payable are simply debited to that account. It is the practice in some cases to carry the contributions to a Superannuation Fund and charge the pensions thereto, any deficiency being debited to the Maintenance Account.

(f) Loan Charges. The loan interest and repayment in respect of the buildings is repayable by the Local Authority who provided the institution, consequently no account of capital outlay, loan indebtedness, etc., will appear in the Mental Hospital Accounts.

(4) Education Accounts.

Education Accounts, which are in all cases subject to the District audit and very often nothing more than the cash receipts and payments, are summarized according to the requirements of the Financial Statement.

The main divisions are—

(a) Elementary Education—

　　Council Schools. Salaries and Maintenance.

　　Council Non-Provided Schools. Salaries and Maintenance.

　　Central Day School and Day Continuation Classes. Salaries and Maintenance.

Schools for Blind, Deaf, Defective and Epileptic Children. Salaries and Maintenance.

School Medical Service.

Administration Expenses.

Truant and Industrial Schools and Detention Homes.

Loan Charges.

(b) Higher and Technical Education—

Polytechnics.

Evening Institutes and Continuation Schools.

Secondary Schools.

Training of Teachers.

Exhibition, Scholarships and Free Places.

The accounts are kept separate and the income is partly derived from Government Grants and by contributions from the respective Rating Funds.

(5) Libraries' Accounts.

By the passing of the Public Libraries Act, 1919, an important alteration has been effected in relation to the accounts.

(a) The old limitation of the 1d. rate has been abolished.

(b) The powers of the Libraries Committee may be transferred to the Education Committee.

(c) The annual subsidy in respect of public libraries may by resolution of the Council be limited to a specified amount : this may be the equivalent of a specified rate or the amount of the annual estimate sanctioned by the Finance Committee.

From a book-keeping standpoint the best course is to treat the libraries accounts in exactly the same way as the accounts of any other committee. It is advisable, however, not to merge the accounts in the Rating Fund chargeable, but to retain the separate fund which has been established.

(6) Overseers' Accounts.

The books to be kept by overseers have been prescribed by Order and are detailed in Chapter III. They are in all cases subject to audit by the District Auditor. The remarkable feature about the Overseers' Accounts is that whilst the books relating to the collection of the Poor Rate are admirably adapted for income and expenditure the whole results are gathered into a so-called " Balance Sheet of the overseers' receipts and payments for the half year ended —————." The certificate at the foot to be signed by the District Auditor is—" I certify that this Balance Sheet is correct."

The return has on the debit side the cash balance brought forward, the amounts received from Poor Rates, Government contribution, rents of property, etc., and on the credit side payments in respect of contribution orders of guardians, police (Metro.), borough councils, etc., and the expenses of overseers in respect of jury lists, valuation expenses, salaries of assistant overseers, etc.

No account is taken of assets or liabilities, consequently the true position is not shown. It is very necessary when making the estimate for the Poor Rate to take into account the collectable arrears of rates, also the amounts owing to other authorities when the previous rate has been insufficient to enable the overseers to meet their demands.

(7) Superannuation Accounts.

Where a pension or superannuation scheme exists, it is necessary (with the exception of mental hospital schemes) to keep separate accounts and credit the fund with contributions from employees (if any) and the contributions from the Local Authority. The former are obtained by deduction from salaries and wages. It is necessary to keep a record of each contributor's contributions and additions, these sometimes being returnable with or without interest on his leaving the service.

The available surplus in the fund is invested from time to time in realizable securities. The fund is generally reported upon by an actuary every five years. There is nothing involving any intricate book-keeping entries, but the enormous amount of detailed work involved may be cut down to some extent by the adoption of up-to-date methods of recording described in a later chapter.

CHAPTER IX

STORES RECORDS AND COST ACCOUNTS

THE accounts relating to the keeping of "Stores" and "Cost" accounts are quite distinct. The practice of many writers and lecturers is to treat them as inseparable, but this leads to considerable confusion. Although it is impossible to have a system of "cost" accounts without adequate stores records it is quite possible to have a system of stores records, although cost accounts, strictly speaking, are not kept.

(1) The Object of Keeping Stores Records.

When a Local Authority carries a stock of materials for any purpose whatever it becomes necessary to keep proper records so as to ensure—

(a) The rating funds and the trading undertakings bear the expenditure on stores used during the financial year.

(b) The prevention of waste or extravagance.

(c) The misappropriation of material.

(d) The prevention of charging to one head of expenditure stores used for another purpose.

(e) An adequate check upon stores disposed of.

(f) Where "cost" accounts are kept—adequate records for charging out the stores used on the different jobs for which cost accounts are required.

(2) The Essential Conditions.

There are three essential conditions to be taken into consideration if the system is to be satisfactory; they are—

(*a*) An efficient control of the stores. This implies a proper place for the materials to be stored and a person responsible for the receipt and issue of stores.

(*b*) Simplicity. Complicated systems defeat their own object. The main function of storekepeers, foremen and workmen consists in the handling and issuing of stores; they are not book-keepers, consequently pardonable errors in carrying out complicated systems may be used as a cover to hide misappropriations.

(*c*) The system must be capable of being incorporated in the main system of accounts. This implies stock-taking and accounting for differences. It also implies that the chief Financial Officer is satisfied that the stores records, which are incorporated, are correctly kept, whether the storekeeper is under his own control or responsible to the head of another department.

(3) The Book-keeping System.

The main books required to be kept are—

(*a*) STORES RECEIVED BOOK. The storekeeper will periodically prepare his requisition for stores required and forward same to the head of his department. When certified, orders are issued from the department on tradesmen for goods required. When the goods are received the items should be entered in detail from the delivery notes into the Stores Received Book. This book may be in tabular form and contain columns for Date, Name of Tradesmen, Description, Quantity, Price, Value, Invoice Number and Posting Folio. The pricing and insertion of the invoice number should be done by the invoice clerk of the department concerned rather than the storekeeper.

(*b*) STORES ISSUED BOOK. Goods should only be obtainable from the storekeeper on presentation of a requisition signed by a responsible person. The Stores Issued Book will be entered up from the requisitions as to quantities. The pricing should be done by the invoice clerk of the department concerned. The book should be ruled with columns for Date, Purpose, Requisition No., Description, Quantity, Price, Folio to Stock Ledger, and Folio to Cost Ledger.

(c) STORES LEDGER. This book will contain accounts of stores classified. Quantities and rates are only posted from the " Received " and " Issued " books. The balance on each account should agree with the actual quantity in stock, subject to certain adjustments.

The above three books contain a record of goods received, issued, and in stock ; the next step is to consider the charging of goods issued to the proper account chargeable, which may be done either—

(1) By the adoption of expenditure analysis columns in the Stores Issued Book into which the items are extended. This method is suitable where the heads of expenditure are not numerous, as, for instance, stores used on a tramway undertaking.

(2) By direct posting from the Stores Issued Book to the Expenditure or Cost Ledger. This method entails a considerable amount of clerical work, but where the number of jobs are numerous it seems to be the most effective.

An alternative method to the one outlined above may be adopted for small authorities where the operations on stores are comparatively few. The Stores Received and Stores Issued Book is dispensed with, the Stock Ledger being adapted to serve the purpose of all three. Goods received are entered direct to the debit of the classified account, and the issues direct to the credit side. It is necessary to have columns on each side for value, and on the issues side analysis columns for accounts to be charged therewith. The serious objection to this method is the difficulty of checking the Ledger with the invoices and the trouble involved in obtaining necessary data for incorporation into the main system of accounts.

There are a few extraordinary transactions which may be mentioned—

(a) RETURN OF STORES INTO STOCK. These should be posted to the debit of the Stock Account in the Stock Ledger and the credit to the job given by way of deduction in the allocation columns of stores issued.

(b) SALE OF GOODS FROM STORE. These should be passed through the Stores Issued Book, posted therefrom to the credit of the particular stock account, and charged out in the allocation to Sundry Sales Account.

(c) STOCKTAKING. This should be done at the end of the financial year, the sheets prepared and quantities entered by the storekeeper from his ledger balance being checked by some independent person with the actual stock. The storekeeper will probably, in addition to his stock accounts in the Ledger, adopt the system of card records in each store bin.

(d) ADJUSTMENT OF DIFFERENCES. The stock accounts must be made to agree with the actual stock, the differences being transferred to an adjustment account which is charged to some general head of expenditure subject to satisfactory explanation.

(4) The Incorporation of Stores Accounts into the Main System.

The whole of the foregoing books mentioned are subsidiary, and it is necessary to get the results periodically into the main accounts of the corporation. The General Ledger should contain an account called " Stores Account" to which is debited through the Purchases Analysis Book all accounts which refer to goods taken to stores. Periodically the Stores Account is credited, through the Journal, with transfers to the respective heads of expenditure according to the totals of the Stores Issued Book. The balance of the Stores Account represents the stock on hand, which should agree with the balances of the Stores Ledger Accounts, duly priced out, after agreement with the actual stocktaking at the end of the year.

(5) Definition of Cost Accounts.

The term " Cost Accounts " is used in connection with accounting for the materials, labour and other expenses incurred in the manufacture of a commodity or commodities or a class of commodities. In its widest application it includes the cost of production as distinct from the prime cost.

Cost Accounts have been grouped into the following—

(a) OUTPUT OR SINGLE COST ACCOUNTS. Applicable to such businesses as breweries, collieries, quarries, mines, etc., in which there is a natural unit of cost, as a barrel of beer brewed or a ton of coal raised.

(b) FACTORY COST ACCOUNTS. These may be the account of the cost of departments, the cost of producing various articles or classes of articles which have no relation to each other, or the cost of each process in the manufacture of any articles.

(c) OPERATING OR WORKING COST ACCOUNTS. Applicable to tramways, gas, water, and electrical undertakings.

(d) CONTRACT OR TERMINAL COST ACCOUNTS. Where the information required is the cost of a contract entered into and the profit or loss thereon. These are applicable to engineers, contractors, builders, etc.

(6) The Object of Keeping Cost Accounts.

It will be seen that from a business point of view the object of keeping cost accounts is to ascertain the cost of production in order that a margin of profit is allowed for in the price to be obtained. Where prices are competitive it is of importance to know how far economies can be effected in the process of manufacture. A third object to be attained is the compilation of sufficient and reliable data on which to base tenders for contracts.

(7) Cost Accounts of a Local Authority.

As it is not intended to deal with cost accounts other than from the aspect of their relationship to Local Authorities, we will leave those commercial groups (*a*) and (*b*), and see how far we are concerned with (*c*) and (*d*).

OPERATING COSTS. Where a Local Authority owns tramways, electricity, gas or water undertakings, the system which requires complete and separate accounts for each provides the data for any information relating to cost. It is assumed that there is a proper Stores Record system in operation. The object is to ascertain the cost of working and for this purpose a unit of cost is selected. In the case of tramways this would be the car mile run ; in gasworks per ton of coal carbonized or per 1,000 ft. of gas sold ; in electricity it may be for the Board of Trade unit generated.

TERMINAL OR CONTRACT COST ACCOUNTS. Where there is a proper Works Department which employs direct labour on all kinds of constructional works, in addition to the numerous jobbing works, some of which are chargeable to private persons, the importance of a good system of costing cannot be over-emphasized.

(8) Expenditure Constituting the Cost.

(*a*) So far as operating costs are concerned the expenditure is represented by the whole of the charges debited to the Revenue Account. These charges in respect of a municipal trading undertaking will differ from those of a company on account of the charges for interest on capital and loan repayments and Sinking Fund charges being included, in place of the charges for depreciation.

(*b*) Terminal costs of works by direct labour.

In some instances the engineer puts in a competitive tender with contractors for certain work to be done and the committee concerned will generally accept the lowest. It is therefore important that the estimate of cost should contain at least all similar charges on which the contractor bases his estimate. It should be noted that the sanctioning authority generally stipulates that no amount shall be included in expenditure out of loans in respect of permanent workmen or officials. This, however, should not prevent the inclusion of all indirect charges when preparing estimates.

It is more important still that when the work is completed, the actual cost should be ascertained irrespective of the estimate.

The expenditure will be in respect of—

(a) DIRECT CHARGES. Materials purchased and sent direct to the job. Materials charged out through the store. Labour of workmen employed on the job. Plant used on the job. Carriage of materials.

(b) INDIRECT CHARGES. Apportionable wages. Apportionable depot charges. Administration expenses.

It is not proposed to discuss the pros and cons of the various methods of apportioning indirect charges. These matters are not decided by the book-keeper; he must know, however, how to make the necessary entries for each method. The following methods may be adopted—

(a) By apportioning the whole of the indirect charges during a period over each job in the ratio that its expenditure bears to the total expenditure.

(b) By an apportionment of indirect charges according to the cost of labour on each job.

(c) By charging each job with an amount equal to a fixed percentage of the value of materials used, or the cost of labour, or on the total of both.

(9) Book-keeping Records.

An account for each job, which is given a distinctive number, will be opened in a special ledger. This may be ruled in columnar form with columns on the debit side for Date, Particulars, Folio, Materials, Wages, Establishment Charges and Total. The credit side should have Date, Particulars, Folio and Amount.

(a) MATERIALS FROM STORE. These will be posted direct from the Stores Issued Book described in the Stores Record System.

(b) MATERIALS CHARGED DIRECT. Some advocate the posting of such items through the Stores Records ; in such case the entries will be as above. If they are not passed through stores, the entries may be posted in detail from the miscellaneous column in the Purchases Analysis Journal, the total of such items being treated in the main system.

(c) WAGES OF WORKMEN. The wages sheets must be dissected according to the time records and the items posted to each job therefrom. The total of such wages will be shown in the Jobbing Works column of the Wages Analysis Book.

(d) PLANT. Sundry articles may be charged direct, in which case the procedure will be as in (b). Apportionable charges will, when calculated, be journalized and posted therefrom to each job.

(e) CARRIAGE AND HAULAGE. Most of these charges will be apportionable and treated in the same manner as in (d).

(f) DEPOT CHARGES AND ADMINISTRATION EXPENSES. These will be treated in a similar manner to (e); the information from which the Journal entries are written up will be provided from the control accounts attached to the main system.

(g) SUNDRY CREDITS. Where stores are returned from the job these will be posted to the credit of the job from the Stores Received Book.

The Job Ledger and the Journal are subsidiary books, but the Ledger when posted is capable of being balanced by the addition of a total account and its correctness ascertained. The whole of the jobs would then be taken out on a Summary Sheet and classified as to—

Expenditure out of loans.

Expenditure for departments chargeable to specified funds.

Expenditure recoverable from private persons.

This information will be required for making the necessary entries and transfers in the main system.

(10) Incorporation into the Main System.

The accounts to be operated upon in the Main System which should be attached to some specific fund, say the General District Fund, are as follows—

(a) WAGES ACCOUNT. This is debited with the total wages paid each week. At the end of the financial year, or periodically, it will be credited with transfers to the respective heads of expenditure according to the Wages Analysis, the wages in respect of Cost Jobs being credited and taken to a Works Account in total. This latter amount will agree in total with the items journalized in detail and posted to the Jobbing Ledger.

(b) STORES ACCOUNT. This is an account in total of all materials passing through the Stores Records. It shows stock on hand at commencement, and purchases on the debit side. It is credited with transfers for stores used on ordinary maintenance and on jobs. The balance at the close of the year represents the value of stock on hand.

(c) HAULAGE ACCOUNT. Where the Local Authority owns its own wagons, etc., this account will be debited in respect of all charges for materials, labour, depreciation, etc. The total expenditure is apportioned according to the agreed charge, any profit on the account being taken to reduce the charges falling upon the ordinary maintenance accounts.

(*d*) PLANT ACCOUNT. This account has, for its debit, value of plant at commencement and purchases during year. Transfers are credited in respect of plant used, usually taken on a percentage basis. The balance will represent the value of plant on hand, and should agree with the valuation.

(*e*) WORKS ACCOUNTS. The whole of the operations are brought to the debit of this account and the final figures transferred to the respective heads of expenditure in the main system. It will be seen that the accounts for wages, haulage, stores and plant have been closed with the exception of the balances on the two latter accounts. As this Works Account contains a summary of the Jobbing Works the details are set out below.

The entries to the debit will be—

Wages   transferred from Wages Account.
Stores   ,,   ,,   Stores Account.
Plant   ,,   Plant Account.
Haulage   ,,   ,,   Haulage Account.
Administration Charges.
Proportion of Salaries   ⎫ Transferred from the re-
Interest   ⎬ spective accounts to which
Depot Charges   ⎭ they are originally debited.

The above entries constitute all the charges for expenditure in connection with the works executed.

The credits will consist of transferring the whole of the above expenditure to the proper accounts as under—

Transfers in respect of expenditure on works carried out, viz.—

TRAMWAYS FUND. Repairs to track.

PRIVATE STREET WORKS. High Street.

WATER WORKS FUND. Laying mains.

CAPITAL ACCOUNT. Sanction £1,000 streets improvements.

SUNDRY PERSONS.   Sundry works recoverable.

The credit should be set out in detail, either in the Ledger or in the Journal, giving in columnar form the wages, materials, plant and establishment expenses.

The information necessary to make the above transfers will be taken from the Jobbing Works summary previously mentioned.   The system outlined is not the only one in operation, but it has the merit of not being inconsistent with the principles laid down and in addition, has, to the author's knowledge, been successfully applied to the cost accounts of a corporation for many years.

(11) Operating Costs.

For the purpose of ascertaining the cost of working, no accounts are required other than those kept to supply the information for the Revenue Account of a trading undertaking.   The information required is the relationship of the expenditure, in detail and in total, to the selected unit.   If, for instance, it is the car mile of a tramway, the statistical records of the traffic department should furnish the total car miles run.   The total of the expenditure is divided by that figure which would give the total operating cost per car mile.   Each head of expenditure is merely the proportion of such total.

The results obtained in respect of the trading undertakings are used for the following purposes—

(a) Comparisons with other similar undertakings.

(b) To fix the basis for charges or fares.

(c) To emphasize waste in a particular item of expenditure in order to effect economies.

In the case of mental hospitals the cost per head per week of each patient must be ascertained in order to fix the charges payable by the guardians and other institutions.

There are other instances of costs required, for instance, the cost per load of dust refuse removed by the Dust

Collection Department or the cost per ton of material destroyed by the dust destructor. The application of the unit basis, the comparison of charges, one year with another, or the utilization of percentages, will give the required information; this, however, cannot strictly be said to be within the province of book-keeping.

CHAPTER X

(1) Depreciation.

To DEFINE depreciation is difficult, but for practical purposes it may be taken to mean the reduction in the exchangeable value of assets. Some writers limit the definition to wasting assets only, holding that Stock Exchange securities and the like are not wasting assets.

This shrinkage in the value of an asset arises from various causes—

(*a*) By wear and tear consequent upon its employment.

(*b*) By effluxion of time as in the case of a lease.

(*c*) By obsolescence, as in the case of some kinds of machinery.

(*d*) By a fall in the market price of investments.

This latter cause is not usually included, as it may only be a temporary shrinkage due to fluctuations of the market.

The necessity for making adequate charges in the accounts for depreciation is due to the fact that the loss is incident to the use of an asset for the purposes of earning revenue. It is a part of the cost of making profits, and as such should be charged against the revenue derived from its use.

There is no easy rule for determining what the shrinkage in value has been during a given period, and none can be correct which does not take into consideration the following factors—

(*a*) The original cost of the asset.

- 80

(*b*) The probable cost of repairs and renewals.

(*c*) The estimated life of the asset.

(*d*) The scrap value at the end of its life.

These factors are all subject to special considerations according to circumstances. There may be a wide difference between original cost and original value ; there is a distinction between repairs and renewals which is not often taken into account ; the life of an asset, although estimated from experience, varies according to circumstances in every case ; the scrap value of a machine has been known to exceed the original cost ; it is therefore unwise to dogmatize on this subject. The commercial accountant has to see if any provision has been made for depreciation, and if so, to consider whether, in his opinion, the amount provided is sufficient.

In commercial accounts depreciation is considered in its relationship to three things—

(*a*) The loss incurred by the use of the asset in earning profits.

(*b*) The valuation of the asset as stated on the Balance Sheet.

(*c*) The necessity of replacing the asset when its usefulness or value is nil.

In the accounts of Local Authorities the application of the commercial arguments for an adequate provision to be made for depreciation is somewhat modified owing to two important differences—

(*a*) So far as the Rating Funds are concerned, there is no question of using assets for making profits.

(*b*) There is a legal obligation imposed upon Local Authorities to repay out of revenue the capital money raised for the purchase of the asset within the period of the sanction. The period is generally supposed to coincide with the probable life of the asset.

It will be seen that some distinction must be made

between Rating Funds and trading undertakings, and the methods adopted and the reasons for their adoption are—

(a) FOR RATING FUNDS. The Revenue Accounts being debited with the annual charges for loan repayments this is considered as sufficient. The replacement of assets will then be provided out of new loans, but as the old loans have been extinguished the financial position is the same as in a company where a depreciation fund has been built up to replace the asset without the issue of new capital. ✗

(b) FOR TRADING UNDERTAKINGS. Considerable controversy has taken place in respect of the different methods of dealing with the question of depreciation. They are stated below for what they are worth—

(1) To charge against revenue in addition to loan repayments a sum sufficient to cover loss by depreciation. The ultimate result of this method will be, if we assume that the life of the asset coincides with the loan period, that at the end of such life the original loan will have been paid off and sufficient reserve created in the business to renew the asset at the same original price without recourse to further loans.

(2) To charge against revenue a sum sufficient to cover depreciation, such sum being carried to the credit of a Depreciation Fund and the loan repayments debited thereto instead of to the Revenue Account. If the period of the loans coincides with the life of the assets this is merely playing with accounts. The effect would be the same as charging loan repayments only to revenue without any reference to depreciation. It might be, however, that the amount set aside for depreciation is insufficient to cover the repayment of loans. The result of the method is that the asset would have to be replaced out of fresh borrowings. The objection to this method is that it strains the principles of book-keeping. A Depreciation Fund is a provision for the renewal of an asset, but if it is

utilized for another purpose—that of repayment of loans—it should at least be correctly named " Redemption Fund."

(3) To charge nothing against Revenue Account for depreciation, on the assumption that the contribution for loan repayments, which must be charged thereto, is equivalent to the provision for depreciation. The result attained here is, that if the asset is useless when the loan is repaid it can be replaced out of fresh borrowings.

The last method is the one generally adopted, and as it does not possess the fallacies of the second method nor burden the undertaking with a double charge against profits like the first, it may be considered as a commercial proposition—

(*a*) The necessity for replacing the asset at the end of its life is met by the ability of the Local Authority to raise fresh loans when the original loans have been repaid, or even earlier.

(*b*) The loss incurred by the use of the asset in earning profits, although not charged against profits, is equalized by the charge for loan repayments, which a commercial undertaking has not to bear, the financial result in both cases being the same.

(*c*) The question of the valuation of the asset as stated on the Balance Sheet must be considered from the standpoint that the Balance Sheet of a Local Authority is prepared on the Double Account System and that there is no question of possible liquidation. There is some doubt as to whether many items of expenditure out of loans may be classed as assets at all, so that the question of valuation is not important. It will be seen that the more important view is the amount of loan indebtedness attached to such outlay.

RENEWAL FUNDS. In many cases where no attempt is made to provide for loss by depreciation reserves are created for the purpose of maintaining the assets in a

state of efficiency. All actual renewals are charged to
this account. It will be seen that this has an important
bearing upon the question of depreciation. Take, for
instance, the case of a tramway track. If the track is
being constantly renewed in parts as required, it is con-
ceivable that at the end of the assumed "life" of the
track it may possibly be in a better condition than
originally. This work of renewal arises out of necessity
and may be said to be a provision for meeting the loss by
depreciation when it occurs.

The question of a suitable allowance for depreciation
arises in the computation of profits assessable to Income
Tax. This will be referred to under the heading of Income
Tax. It also arises in computing the charges for haulage
done by the Corporation. Motor wagons may be purchased and charged to a Suspense Account and a proportion charged each year to Haulage Account, a very
conservative estimate of the probable "life" being taken.

(2) Rate Estimates.

The work of preparing the rate estimates is closely
connected with the keeping of the ledger accounts. The
necessity for analyzing the expenditure in order to provide
the necessary information in respect of each spending
committee has been previously referred to. The estimates
which are in respect of a yearly or half-yearly rate are
prepared in many ways. The following procedure is fairly
general.

(a) HALF-YEARLY ESTIMATES. Assuming that a rate
is to be made to cover the net expenditure for the half-
year ending 30th September, schedules would be prepared
giving in columnar form the actual expenditure for the
corresponding period of the previous year, and the estimates
for the current half-year. This is sent to the head of the
department concerned, who inserts in a third column
the estimate of his requirements. In practice the chief

book-keeper will furnish the information for certain known expenditure, as salaries, rates and taxes, loan charges, etc. The estimate is then submitted to the committee concerned for its approval.

The whole of the approved estimates are then summarized by the chief financial officer, who submits them to the Finance Committee with his report as to the rate required. This committee, will, after modifying the estimates in any way, recommend to the Council the rate to be made.

The amount required to be raised by rate will be the total sum of the estimated net expenditure, to which is added the estimated deficiency at the 31st March. If there is an estimated surplus it will, of course, be deducted.

The estimated surplus is the amount by which the income from rates plus the actual surplus, if any, at the beginning of the half-year, exceeds the revised expenditure. The method of preparing the summary is given in Appendix F.

It will be necessary for the Expenditure Ledgers to be balanced at the 31st December in order to obtain the actual expenditure for the quarter to that date. To this is added the estimated expenditure for the current quarter; this will give the revised estimated expenditure for the current half-year, which is required in order to ascertain the estimated surplus or deficiency.

(b) YEARLY ESTIMATES. As compared with half-yearly estimates yearly ones are not so scientific, and require greater care in their preparation.

Assume that estimates are required for the year ending 31st March, 1946.

The schedules in respect of each committee would be prepared giving in columnar form—

(1) The actual expenditure year to 31st March, 1944.

(2) Current estimate for the year to 31st March, 1945.

(3) Actual expenditure for 9 months to 31st December, 1944.

(4) Estimated expenditure for 3 months to 31st March, 1945.

(5) Revised estimate for the current year—total of (3) and (4).

(6) Estimate for the year ending 31st March, 1946.

The book-keeper will fill in the information for columns (1), (2) and (3).   It is then sent to the head of the department concerned, who will fill in the information required for columns (4) and (6).   The schedules presented to each committee for its approval need not contain columns (3) and (4) as this is merely a method of providing the information for column (5).

The differences between the two methods are—

(a) The half-yearly estimates are based on the actual expenditure for the corresponding period, whilst the yearly estimates are based on the revised current estimate.

(b) The yearly method is open to the objection that, owing to the necessity for making a revised estimate of the current year, which is not subject to the approval of the committees, figures may be manipulated.

PERIODICAL RETURNS OF EXPENDITURE AGAINST ESTIMATES.   It is the practice in some towns for the committees to require monthly statements showing the progress of expenditure as compared with the estimate. The object of this is to exercise some control in order to prevent estimates being overspent.

The object is excellent but the difficulties of providing the information will be apparent.

The information of expenditure to date is prepared in different ways, the following being typical—

(a) The total of accounts previously passed for payment plus those being presented to the committee are taken to represent the expenditure to date.

(*b*) The above total plus any expenditure which can only be estimated.

(*c*) The total of the official orders issued by each department plus certain expenditure, as for rates, taxes, gas, etc., for which no orders are issued. In order to obtain this information, counterfoils of all official orders are sent to the Accountant's Department. The department concerned states the estimated cost of each order and the head of expenditure chargeable. This information is posted to a memo. book ruled with columns for the respective heads of expenditure.

Any method which is adopted depends absolutely upon the state of efficiency obtaining in the ledger department.

(3) Income Tax.

The assessment of Local Authorities for Income Tax is highly technical and has been exhaustively treated in *Income Tax in Relation to Local Authorities*, by F. Ogden Whiteley and Wm. Whittingham. The student is referred to this text-book.

It is anticipated that in the near future certain alterations in the law will be made. At the present time the general principles in operation are—
UNDER SCHEDULE A.

(*a*) On property owned and occupied by the authority; this is generally known as the Landlord's Tax.

(*b*) On property occupied but not owned by the authority. The authority acts as collecting agents but may recover the tax by deducting it from the next payment of rent.
UNDER SCHEDULE B.

In respect of lands in the occupation of the authority. It is known as the Farmer's Tax and is generally imposed in respect of Sewage Farms.
UNDER SCHEDULE C.

In respect of interest upon investments in Government and Colonial securities.

UNDER SCHEDULE D.

In respect of bank interest, interest on loans, etc.

In respect of profits of the trading undertakings.

The three main points to bear in mind in respect of the preparation of the Income Tax Statement showing the net liability of the corporation are—

(*a*) That full advantage is taken of all allowances chargeable against the profits of the trading undertakings, such as proportion of establishment expenses, etc.

(*b*) That all other " set offs " are properly brought into account in addition to the " set off " from the trading undertaking allowed against the Rating Fund assessment. It should be part of the chief book-keeper's duty to see that a register is correctly entered up showing all taxes paid whether by deduction or otherwise and all tax deducted from interest on loans, etc.

(*c*) That with regard to the trading undertakings the proper allowance for depreciation is obtained.

(4) Wages and Deductions therefrom.

A considerable amount of work is thrown upon the staff of the Finance Department in connection with the payment of wages and salaries. The deductions in many cases comprise most of the following—

(*a*) National Health Insurance.

(*b*) Unemployment Insurance.

(*c*) Superannuation Fund Contributions.

(*d*) Income Tax deductions (Staff Scheme).

(*e*) Deductions for Savings Certificates.

In addition to the work involved, information is required by the Inspector of Taxes as to the annual salaries and quarterly wages for each man liable to tax. It will be found advisable to keep a salaries book ruled for each month in respect of salaries, and for all other cases a card record of the weekly earnings.

There is no particular difficulty presented, but the student is reminded that the formulation of any good system for the payment of wages must take into consideration the immense amount of work entailed with respect to deductions and the information required by the Inspector of Taxes.

(5) Preparation and Form of Balance Sheets.

There is a great diversity of opinion as to the form of a Balance Sheet. An attempt was made by the Institute of Municipal Treasurers to remedy the obvious defect of publishing Balance Sheets for similar undertakings in various forms which make comparisons difficult. The standardized forms published by the Council of the Institute, although not adopted generally, have served as useful models.

The Double Account System, which has for its object the division of the Balance Sheet into two portions, the first relating to loans and expenditure thereout, and the second portion to the ordinary Revenue Account balances, has been prescribed by the Board of Trade for electricity undertakings. The reason for this method of division applies to the Balance Sheets of every fund of a Corporation so that there is no objection to one main feature being applicable to all.

The same results can be obtained if the capital portion of the Balance Sheet is sub-totalled instead of the balance being carried from one portion to another, and this form is accepted by the Board of Trade in lieu of the prescribed form.

There are one or two rules which may be observed with advantage when considering the form of a Balance Sheet—

(a) The assets should be grouped properly under their respective classes.

(b) There should be a sub-division of classes of assets sufficient to present a clear view of the state of affairs.

(c) The assets should be marshalled in some logical order, starting with the fixed assets and following on with the floating assets in their natural order of realization.

(d) Tangible and intangible assets should be separately shown.

(e) So far as possible any change in the book value of assets should be recorded on the Balance Sheet by addition or deduction.

There are one or two minor points which the student should settle in his mind one way or the other—

(a) The sides of the Balance Sheet should not be headed "Liabilities" and "Assets," the natural conclusion being that all items falling under those respective headings are such.

(b) Capital expenditure should be set out in columnar form, giving the outlay at commencing, outlay during the year, and total to date on each respective head.

(c) Loans outstanding should contain the details of the stock represented in the amount owing to the Loans Fund.

(d) In the place of "Excess of Assets and Capital Outlay over Liabilities" it is suggested "Provision made to date towards Capital Outlay."

These are the writer's own opinions and the underlying reason for stating them is to emphasize the fact that a Balance Sheet should be as intelligible as possible to members of the Council and ratepayers.

The Aggregate Balance Sheet is a summary in Balance Sheet form of all the Balance Sheets of a Corporation and should represent the general financial position. It should not contain any items which are not to be found on any specific Balance Sheet. The writer prefers the form set out in the Appendix, this being convenient for grouping the items in a way that can be traced to the specific Balance Sheet. The Appendix contains a series of Balance Sheets which are summarized into an Aggregate Balance Sheet.

(6) The Form of Published Accounts.

The published accounts of Local Authorities are perhaps the best illustration of the need for some attempt at uniformity.

The differences exist in relation to two things—the contents and the order of the contents.

There is a certain minimum of information which any abstract of accounts should contain, viz.—

(a) In respect to each fund.

Revenue Account.

Details of Capital Expenditure.

Balance Sheet.

(b) The Aggregate Balance Sheet.

(c) Report of the Financial Officer.

(d) Report of the Auditors.

The following information is desirable—

(a) Statement of Loan Borrowings and Outstanding Debt.

(b) Tables of Rateable Value, Population, Rates made, etc., covering a period of one year.

(c) Local Trust Accounts and Overseers' Accounts.

An examination of a number of abstracts will suggest that the order of contents is governed by the order in which each fund is balanced. This is not a very good method to adopt.

The following order is suggested as being a practical solution based as near as possible on a logical sequence—

(a) The Report of the Financial Officer.

(b) The Aggregate Balance Sheet.

(c) The Revenue Accounts and Balance Sheet of each Rating Fund.

(d) The Revenue Accounts and Balance Sheet of each Trading Undertaking.

(e) The Revenue Accounts and Balance Sheets of other Funds, including Education and Mental Hospital Accounts.

(*f*) Stock Redemption Funds and Balance Sheets.

(*g*) Overseers and other Local Accounts.

(*h*) Loan Statements and statistical information.

(*i*) Auditors' report.

It will be noticed that the Aggregate Balance Sheet is put first. The reason for this is that it shows the general financial position of the Corporation and is closely related to the report of the Financial Officer. From the public readers' standpoint the report and the Aggregate Balance Sheet contain a bird's-eye view of the financial position.

The Rating Funds Revenue Accounts, in addition to the detailed accounts, might be set out in summary form on one page.

Every fund which is financed through the Loans Fund should precede that fund ; this will bring the Education Accounts and the Visiting Committees Accounts before and not after it.

It is advisable to make the abstract as concise as possible and to eliminate anything in the nature of padding.

CHAPTER XI

1. Tabular Ledgers.
2. Loose Leaf Ledgers.
3. Card Systems.
4. Slip System.

5. Adding Machines and Calculators.
6. Filing Systems.

A SKILLED book-keeper in order to put his knowledge into effect should, in addition to being thoroughly conversant with the underlying principles of book-keeping and the particular application of those principles to the class of accounts required by a Local Authority, possess some information about modern methods which can be adapted to the requirements of the book-keeper.

It has been thought advisable to make one or two suggestions in this volume owing to the fact that the work of the book-keeper in many places has been hampered by prejudice and foolish objection to change of any kind. There are many offices even to-day where the ledgers are of the most elementary description. On the other hand it is not unusual to find in other offices new things being adopted simply because they are new, without regard to their proper use and economy. It is well before adopting anything new to apply one or two rules in order to make a wise decision—

(a) Will the new device or altered form economize the cost of printing and stationery?

(b) Will its adoption have the effect of reducing the amount of clerical work entailed?

(c) Will the result be a more efficient record of accounts?

We have passed the day when mere academic discussions are the only result of new ideas; the question of advantages or disadvantages of any particular method need only be raised, not in regard to its general application but to its particular application to the specific requirements. Some of the things to be mentioned later are not by any means new except where they have never been used before. I should like to say a word as to the advisability of using extreme caution inasmuch as the application of a right method to a wrong purpose may entail loss of money and general dissatisfaction.

The primary books of account consisted of ledgers and cash books with single columns for cash, and in order to cope with the increasing number of accounts to be recorded, they developed on the old lines to bulky and unwieldy volumes which, though impressive looking, were exceedingly difficult to handle.

(1) Tabular Ledgers.

One of the first improvements designed to remedy the ancient system was the extension of the page by the addition of several columns. Columnar books are now a recognized feature of any office : general examples one could mention are the Rate Book, the Electricity Consumers' Rental, Expenditure Analysis Books, etc. The effect of the adoption of this principle in the Electricity Consumers' Rental is that it is possible to get as many as thirty Consumers' Accounts on one page instead of one, without any corresponding loss of information. It is not necessary to labour the point ; this principle has an immense advantage where it can be properly applied and it is only necessary to point out one instance where there still seems to be a variety of opinions and diversity of practice. In many corporations for each account there is a separate Pass Book at the bank and a separate Cash Book in the office ; the argument put forward to justify this seems to be that it puts certain work upon the bank clerks which would otherwise be done in the office, and that it facilitates the calculation of bank interest. It has, however, been found to work very well in practice to reduce the number of accounts at the bank and in their place to adopt a columnar Pass Book, the analysis of receipts and payments being performed in the office of the Local Authority. The Cash Books are combined with similar columns; this has the effect of dispensing with an undue number of books to be kept by one particular clerk and incidentally it pools the cash at the bank in respect of the cash accounts amalgamated. In large corporations the work entailed in apportioning bank interest already exists, it being the practice of the bank to keep a Daily Balance Book in respect of all the accounts, the interest being charged or allowed upon the net total. This illustration will serve our purpose in pointing out that the mere evasion of work is no good reason for not adopting the principle, and that it certainly does not tend to efficiency.

(2) Loose Leaf Ledgers.

A Loose Leaf Ledger has a permanent binder from which the leaves can be released when necessary. There have been very strong objections made to its use upon account of the detachability of its leaves. It is very difficult to ascertain from those who object why anyone in a large office should wish to remove the leaves, but assuming that the object were to facilitate fraud this can be adequately safeguarded against by a proper control of the ledgers and the locking devices. These ledgers are eminently suitable for those groups of accounts which can be sub-divided into accounts which are practically continuous and those which are temporary. Tradesmens' Creditors Ledgers are a good example of this. Instead of a bound book with balances being carried forward to different pages, each account, however large it may grow, will remain in its original place in the index by the substitution of additional leaves when necessary. The other advantage is that Dead Accounts and dead pages of

Live Accounts may be removed periodically, the benefit of which will be apparent to any book-keeper.

It is curious that the greatest objection has been raised against the adoption of Loose Leaf Books for cash records. Generally speaking, there does not seem much advantage to be claimed by adopting the principle for a Cash Book, except in exceptional circumstances, where it is necessary to have the loose leaf for the purpose of recording the cash items, as will be referred to later on.

(3) Card Systems.

The principle underlying the use of Card Ledgers is the same as that for Loose Leaf Ledgers, the cards in the place of loose leaves being kept in drawers. This method has been adopted for electricity consumers in some places, but it appears more convenient for records which are not strictly part of the main system. For instance, records of wages paid to each individual which are required for income tax returns may be conveniently kept by this method. Practically all the necessary records which must be kept in connection with Motor Car Registration and Local Taxation licences will be found most convenient in this form.

(4) Slip System.

This system of book-keeping has been largely adopted in commercial businesses of recent years. The principle is that of using a slip or docket as a medium from which original entries may be posted direct to the accounts in the Ledger. This practice has been adopted by banks for many years. In commercial houses the slips, which are numbered, are attached to the sales notes and the posting therefrom made direct to the Debtors Ledgers and the credit taken to the Sales Account. This has the effect of cutting out of use the Sales Journal.

In connection with Municipal Accounts the method can be applied to Tradesmen's Accounts, the posting being made direct to the credit of the Personal Account and the debit direct to the Expenditure Account. This has the effect of dispensing with the Expenditure Analysis Book. A method which is even shorter, although it infringes the rules of double entry book-keeping, is to enter the cash payments book from the slip attached to the invoices and debit the expenditure accounts. This cuts out the personal accounts, it being claimed that the invoices themselves, which are filed, constitute the personal record. Although it does not appear likely that the slip system will ever be adopted to any large extent in connection with the accounts of local authorities it is somewhat difficult to show why it should not be, in the face of the advantages claimed, viz.—

(a) The reduction in the number of books required.

(b) The consequent economy in labour and printing.

(c) The ready reference to the original invoices.

(d) The reduction of the possibility of error, there being no intermediate entries between the Ledger and the invoice.

(e) The facilities for promptly posting the items.

It must be said, however, that this method cannot be applied to all classes of accounts, and need only be considered in comparison with other methods which claim the same advantages.

(5) Adding Machines and Calculators.

There is no work performed in a book-keeping office which is more generally disliked or more costly to perform than additions and calculations without the aid of machinery. One would naturally conclude that any machine which required no mental effort to work, which was absolutely accurate, and which claimed as its chief advantage speed, would have been adopted universally.

Before adopting an adding machine the chief thing to be considered is whether there is sufficient work to justify its purchase. This depends upon what use can be made of it, and the following suggestions are made from experience—

(a) RATE WORK. In any town having 10,000 rate assessments the work of the rate staff in adding and balancing the various columns of the rate books can be enormously reduced.

(b) LEDGER WORK. A very useful work which can be done is the extraction of ledger balances at any time. A machine which will list the figures of both debits and credits and give the totals with one pull of the crank will appeal to any book-keeper who has had to work on the old method.

(c) CASH RECEIPTS. We will assume, for instance, that the collection of the rates and other income is centralized, and the whole of it comes in direct to the Town Hall. A very large percentage will be received through the post and in this connection very useful work can be performed with the aid of an adding machine. Take for instance the rates. The letters when opened will be sorted into various groups, those relating to rates being one. The demand notes which generally accompany the remittances are handed over to the adding machine operator. By an adaptation of the loose leaf system for the Rates Cash Book it is possible to place the leaf in the machine and to type thereon the Assessment Number, Amount of Poor Rate, General District Rate, Water Rate, Costs and Total. The machine will not only cross cast each line but give the final total. In the meantime the cheques, etc., are being entered up in the paying-in books, and on completion the totals of the Cash Sheet and the paying-in sheet are agreed. The money is then paid straight into the bank and the Cash Sheet with the demand notes, etc., sent to the Rates Office.

The advantages will be apparent to anyone who has been struggling with the old method. The cash books are legibly written up by someone who does not touch the cash, the money is paid promptly into the bank and the postings are subsequently made and the receipts issued promptly and in a manner which will effectually prevent misappropriations and fraud.

A calculator differs from an adding machine in so far that it does not print and that it is adapted for calculations involving not only addition but division, multiplication and subtraction. It can be used for checking extensions of items on accounts and in conjunction with an adding machine is invaluable for purposes of statistical work involving averages and percentages.

In addition to the foregoing there are numerous devices for saving work and ensuring accuracy which, though they are not directly connected with the work of book-keeping, have the general effect of maintaining the efficiency of the office. The addressing machine, for instance, can be made to act as a check upon accounts rendered.. These may, therefore, be considered, in addition to the general advantages claimed for them, as automatic checks upon the book-keeper.

(6) Filing Systems.

In order to save confusion and delay it is absolutely necessary that some attention should be given to the method of filing. The old system of tying up accounts when paid into brown paper parcels is hopeless from an efficiency point of view. Accounts when passed by the respective committees are handed to the book-keeper for analysis and entry, and very often afterwards are seen lumbering up the office in unsightly heaps. There are one or two things which are often forgotten—

(a) Invoices are frequently required for reference in cases of dispute.

(b) Accounts rendered go astray and duplicates may be required.

(c) The whole are required for production at audit.

It will be seen, therefore, that the system required is one that will enable the book-keeper readily to find an invoice or account when required, and in addition all correspondence in relation to the accounts.

The Slip System is in itself a method of filing invoices in a way which is excellent. In practice it is usual to fix the monthly lots of accounts together in the order of submission to committee ; when an account is required this necessitates a reference to some book in order to find it. Where personal accounts are kept there should be no difficulty in filing the invoices away in alphabetical or ledger order.

It has not been thought necessary by the writer to do more than impress upon the book-keeper that the practical side of book-keeping is necessarily associated with methods and machinery, just as the art of the painter is associated with the best methods of mixing the colours, etc. The " qualification " of a book-keeper must include a knowledge of methods and the reasons for their adoption.

CHAPTER XII

1. The Scope of the Examination.
2. Books recommended for Study.
3. A Review of the Examination Questions on Book-keeping.

THE finance office of a Local Authority offers to the youth who enters therein two alternatives—a monotonous, unimaginative, humdrum existence with the prospect of regular employment at a moderate salary, or progress and ultimate attainment to the position of chief Financial Officer. It all depends upon his willingness to study and qualify.

There is no doubt that a junior clerk is well advised to first of all read and sit for the book-keeping examination of the Chamber of Commerce or the Society of Arts. This with due attention to commercial arithmetic, will give him an immense advantage in the early stages of his career ; he may then with every confidence turn his attention to the examinations of the Institute of Municipal Treasurers and Accountants.

(1) The Scope of the Examination.

The examinations which have for their object that of equipping and training financial officers are divided into two sections, the Primary and the Final examination.

Questions are set in the following subjects—
Arithmetic and Algebra (Primary only).
Book-keeping and Accounts.
Local Authority Finance.
Auditing.
Mercantile and Municipal Law.
Economics and Statistics (Final only).

We are in this volume concerned only with the second subject, that of book-keeping. It is pointed out in the syllabus that for the Primary Examination a sound knowledge of the principles of double entry book-keeping and their practical application to the various accounts (including trading undertakings) of Local Authorities will be required. For the Final Examination a thorough practical knowledge of the higher branches of book-keeping and accountancy will be required, and of *modern* methods of keeping and preparing accounts of all classes of Local Authorities, including trading undertakings.

It will be recognized that these requirements have influenced the writer.

(2) Books Recommended for Study.

The books recommended for study include Allcock's *Municipal Accounts*, Eckersley's *Urban District Council Accounts*, and Collins's *Organization and Audit of Local Authorities' Accounts*. The first two deal mainly with explanations of forms of accounts, in so far as they touch book-keeping as a subject, and the latter contains an excellent compendium of the many systems in operation, reports of Departmental Committees, together with a detailed system of audit control.

The remainder are publications on commercial book-keeping which only incidentally refer to the accounts of local authorities.

In order to help the student, perhaps the better plan is to show him what he actually must know and the best means of obtaining that information without waste of time spent in skimming all sorts of books.

It must be remembered, however, that a knowledge of the principles of double entry is required, and this is tested by questions set in commercial book-keeping. The student may choose his own text-books in this subject, of which there is a plentiful supply, but it is in the practical application of those principles to the accounts of Local Authorities that he may find some difficulty in obtaining his information.

(3) A Review of the Examination Questions on Book-keeping.

In looking through the past examination papers some useful information on this subject may be gathered. The following are a few points worth considering—

(*a*) Exercises involving the preparation of Profit and Loss or Revenue Accounts and Balance Sheets.

These may be classified into—

(1) COMMERCIAL. These have included the accounts of a sole trader, partnership accounts and the accounts of joint stock companies. It is quite obvious that a knowledge of commercial accounts is required to answer such questions and the student can make his own choice of a suitable text-book. It is important, however, that he should not neglect this side of the subject and it is for that reason that I have previously urged the advantage of sitting for the examinations of the Society of Arts and Chamber of Commerce.

(2) TRADING UNDERTAKINGS. These relate to gas, water, electricity, tramways, etc., and may be studied from the standpoint of the differences which exist in the accounts of Local Authorities' undertakings and those owned by Commercial Companies. The information concerning the latter can be obtained from special publications, but most books on advanced book-keeping contain all that is necessary. For information concerning the former much can be obtained from the published abstracts of accounts of representative towns. The differences in the form of accounts consist mainly in connection with the Capital Accounts and Loan Repayments.

(3) RATING AND OTHER FUNDS. There has only been one way to get the information necessary to answer questions

involving Balance Sheets on such subjects as District Funds, Loan Fund or Lunatic Asylums, and that is from actual experience or the study of published abstracts of accounts. This is of course supplemented by such information as can be given by a coach.

(b) Questions involving a knowledge of the theory of double entry book-keeping.

Certain problems are stated and the student is asked to give the necessary book entries. The theoretical know-ledge required can be acquired from the study of any up-to-date work on book-keeping. The difficulty, however, lies in the application of general principles to particular instances which only apply in municipal accounts. It is here that the close connection with commercial accounting is to be seen. The student must have the imagination to find municipal examples by which to test and apply the rules given in commercial accounts.

(c) Questions involving the knowledge of Local Government Law.

Unquestionably the greatest difficulty in connection with the study of municipal accounts is the acquisition of the necessary information in order to correctly apply the legal restrictions. Generally speaking, every act of a local authority must be sanctioned by some Act of Parliament, Order in Council, or Regulations issued under an Act. The book-keeper must have a working knowledge of the financial provisions of such Acts, etc., in so far as they bear upon the following points—

(a) The fund out of which expenses are to be defrayed.

(b) The limit imposed upon such expenditure.

(c) The prescribed order (if any) in which the accounts must be prepared and submitted.

(d) The powers of raising rates.

(e) The extent of borrowing powers and the limit of capital expenditure.

The writer has intentionally eliminated as much as

possible of this legal element in the previous chapters in order to present a statement of the book-keeping points quite apart from statutory conditions. Some questions demand of the student specific details of certain Acts being committed to memory. Take the following—" What are the main items of Receipt and Payment in the Exchequer Contribution Account of a County Borough ? Briefly explain each item." The only way to be prepared for such a question is by taking the Local Government Act of 1888, and amending Acts so far as they relate thereto, and making notes of all the financial provisions in detail and committing them to memory.

In practice, however, no one trusts to memory and it is of extreme importance that in addition to a general knowledge of the financial provisions of the local statutes one should very definitely know where to refer in all points of dispute. The main statutes which relate to the constitution, power and duties of various Local Authorities in England are as follows—

Municipal Corporations Act, 1882. (All Boroughs.)

Local Government Act, 1894. (Urban Districts, etc.)

Local Government Act, 1888. (Counties and County Boroughs.)

London Government Act, 1899. (Metropolitan Boroughs.)

The Public Health Acts, 1875, etc.

The Public Health (London) Act, 1891.

The Education Acts, 1902–1918.

In addition to the above there are the adoptive Acts, the statutes which regulate the trading undertakings, and a large number of small Acts which may or may not apply to a particular authority. It is also well to remember that many large towns exercise powers under their own local Acts.

The question of the accounts of Local Authorities has been the subject of departmental enquiry, and the publications given on page 106 contain useful information.

Report of Departmental Committee on Accounts of Local Authorities, 1907 (Cd. 3614).

Report of the Joint Committee on Municipal Trading, 1912.

Report of the Select Committee on the application of Sinking Funds in exercise of borrowing power, 1909 (H.C. 193).

Local Authorities Borrowing Powers, 1913 (H.L. 179).

Final Report of the Departmental Committee on Local Taxation, 1914 (Cd. 7315).

With regard to the powers and duties of overseers, all the necessary information will be found in either Knight's or Mackenzie's *Overseers' Manual*. By far the best summary of rates made and expenses chargeable thereto is to be found in the first eighty pages of the appendix to *Minutes of Evidence* (Vol. I), Royal Commission on Local Taxation (C. 8764).

In addition much valuable information has been published from time to time in the shape of lectures delivered to the various students' societies connected with the Institute of Municipal Treasurers.

It may well cause the prospective student to stagger when he contemplates what is before him. I should like to say that although these difficulties, when considered in the bulk at a distance, may appear to be very formidable, they can be surmounted by the steady application of specific study piece by piece. The greatest asset a student can possess is the habit of reasoning out why things are done in such a way. The solution of his queries may not satisfy a reasonable mind as many things are done simply because a certain Act of Parliament says so.

In conclusion the writer is of opinion that there is no legislation existing at the present time which would definitely prevent the application of the principles of double entry book-keeping to the accounts of Local Authorities.

APPENDICES

107

CAPITAL ACCOUNT.

To Consolidated Loans Fund—	Original Allocation. £	Stock Extinguished by Transfer. £	£
1st Issue of 3% Redeemable Stock	100,000	15,000	85,000
2nd do. do. do.	208,500	10,000	198,500
	308,500	25,000	283,500
Transferred Stock—			
3rd Issue			20,000
			303,500
„ *Mortgage Loans Fund—*			
Loans Allocated . .		48,000	
Less Repaid . . .		2,000	
			46,000
„ *Provision made to date towards Capital Outlay—*			
Loans repaid . . .		2,000	
Permanent Works paid for out of Revenue . .		2,000	
Consolidated Loans Fund— Stock Extinguished by Transfer . . .		25,000	
Sinking Funds . .		60,000	
			89,000
			438,500

REVENUE ACCOUNT.

To Sundry Creditors . . .			7,000
„ Cash Overdrawn . . .			3,000
„ Suspense A/c Income Tax .			2,000
„ Revenue Surplus { last account	1,500		
{ for the year	500		
			2,000
			14,000
			£452,500

BALANCE SHEET.

MARCH, 19—.

CAPITAL ACCOUNT.

By *Property and Capital Outlay*	*Outlay at Beginning of Year.*	*Outlay during Year.*	*Total Outlay.*
	£	£	£
Municipal Buildings . .	100,000	—	100,000
Police Stations . . .	35,000	10,000	45,000
Mental Hospitals . .	200,000	—	200,000
Law Courts . . .	25,000	—	25,000
Judges' Lodgings . .	1,000	—	1,000
Costs of Stock Issue . .	2,500	—	2,500
Cost of Local Acts . .	3,000	2,000	5,000
	366,500	12,000	378,500

„ *Consolidated Loans Fund—*

Investments and Cash .   60,000

438,500

REVENUE ACCOUNT.

By Sundry Debtors . .	9,810	
„ Sundry Officers' Petty Cash	25	
„ Suspense Accounts . .	465	
„ Exchequer Contribution A/c	3,700	
		14,000

£452,500

       ELECTRICITY FUND

31st

CAPITAL ACCOUNT.

	Original Allocation.	Stock Extinguished by Transfer.	
To *Consolidated Loans Fund*—	£	£	£
2nd Issue 3% Redeemable Stock	91,500	—	91,500
3rd Issue do. do.	170,500	20,000	150,500
	262,000	20,000	242,000
Transferred Stock—			
1st Issue . . .		15,000	
2nd Issue . . .		10,000	
			25,000
			267,000
,, *Mortgage Loans Fund*—			
Loans Allocated . .		40,000	
Less Repaid . . .		5,000	
			35,000
,, Provision made to date towards Capital Outlay—			
Loans Repaid . . .		5,000	
Permanent Works paid for out of revenue . .		5,000	
Consolidated Loans Fund—			
Stock extinguished by Transfer . . .		20,000	
To Sinking Funds . .		50,000	
			80,000
			382,000

REVENUE ACCOUNT.

To Sundry Creditors—			
Trade Accounts . .	20,000		
Deposit Accounts . .	2,000		
		22,000	
,, Reserve Funds—			
Last Account . .	25,000		
Add Net Profits for year .	5,900		
		30,900	
			52,900
			£434,900

BALANCE SHEET.

MARCH, 19—.

CAPITAL ACCOUNT.

By *Property and Capital Outlay—*	Outlay Beginning of Year.	Outlay during Year.	Total Outlay.
	£	£	£
Land	1,500	—	1,500
Buildings	40,000	5,000	45,000
Machinery and Plant	60,000	2,000	62,000
Direct Current Plant	50,000	—	50,000
Mains	100,000	7,000	107,000
Services	50,000	—	50,000
Meters	2,000	—	2,000
Accumulators	3,000	—	3,000
Instruments	5,000	—	5,000
Tools	4,000	—	4,000
Costs of Issue	2,500	—	2,500
	318,000	14,000	332,000

,, *Consolidated Loans Fund—*
Investments and Cash   50,000

382,000

REVENUE ACCOUNT.

By Debtors—For Current supplied   40,000
,,   Sundry   800
                                                    40,800
,, Stores on hand   12,000
,, Petty Cash in hands of Officers   100
                                                    52,900

£434,900

APPENDIX C.

CONSOLIDATED

BALANCE

31st

3 per cent. Redeemable Stock.	Stock Issued and Transferred.	Stock Transferred.	Balance Outstanding.	
	£	£	£	£
First Issue .	100,000	15,000	85,000	
Second Issue .	300,000	10,000	290,000	
Third Issue .	170,500	20,000	150,500	
Stock Transferred	45,000	—	45,000	
	615,500	45,000		570,500

Redemption Fund—

Balance brought forward	.	.	80,000
Accumulations during year	.	.	30,000
			110,000
			£680,500

Note.—Allocation of Sinking Fund Accumulations—

Borough Fund	.	.	.	60,000
Electricity Fund	.	.	.	50,000
				£110,000

LOANS FUND

SHEET.

MARCH, 19—.

By *Allocation of Loans*—

	£	£
Borough Fund	303,500	
Electricity Fund	267,000	
		570,500

Redemption Fund—

Investments: Loans to other Local Authorities	90,000	
Cash in hand	15,000	
Interest accrued	5,000	
	110,000	

£680,500

8—(1763) 12 pp.

APPENDIX D.

MORTGAGE

BALANCE

31ST

	£
To Sundry Mortgages—	
For balance of loans outstanding secured	
on Mortgage	86,000
Unclaimed Interest Warrants . .	25

£86,025

LOANS FUND

SHEET.

MARCH, 19—.

	£	£
By Balance of Loans Appropriated—		
Borough Fund	46,000	
Electricity Fund	35,000	
		81,000
,, Cash in hand—		
Current Account	5,000	
Interest Account	25	
		5,025
		£86,025

LOAN AND CAPITAL ACCOUNTS.

		£	£	£
Three per cent. Redeemable Stock—	£			
Borough Fund . . .			303,500	
Electricity Fund . . .			267,000	
				570,500
Sundry Mortgagees—				
Borough Fund . . .			46,000	
Electricity Fund . . .			35,000	
Unappropriated . . .			5,000	
				86,000
Provision made to date towards Capital Outlay—				
Loans repaid :				
Borough Fund . .	2,000			
Electricity Fund . .	5,000			
			7,000	
Stock Extinguished by Transfer :				
Borough Fund . .	25,000			
Electricity Fund . .	20,000			
			45,000	
Sinking Funds :				
Borough Fund . .	60,000			
Electricity Fund . .	50,000			
			110,000	
Capital Expenditure out of Revenue :				
Borough Fund . .	2,000			
Electricity Fund . .	5,000			
			7,000	
				169,000
				825,500

REVENUE ACCOUNT.

	£	£
Sundry Creditors :		
Borough Fund . .	7,000	
Electricity Fund . .	22,000	
Mortgage Loans Fund .	25	
		29,025
Reserve Fund :		
Electricity Fund . .		30,900
Cash Overdrawn :		
Borough Fund		3,000
Suspense Account :		
Borough Fund		2,000
Revenue Surplus :		
Borough Fund		2,000
		66,925
		£892,425

BALANCE SHEET.

MARCH, 19—.

LOAN AND CAPITAL ACCOUNTS.

					£	£
Capital Expenditure—						
Borough Fund	.	.	.	.	378,500	
Electricity Fund	.	.	.	.	332,000	
						710,500
Stock Redemption Fund—						
Investments	.	.	.	.	90,000	
Cash in hand	.	.	.	.	15,000	
Interest Accrued	.	.	.	.	5,000	
						110,000
						820,500

REVENUE ACCOUNT.

Sundry Debtors :					
Borough Fund	.	.	9,810		
Electricity Fund	.	.	40,800		
Stores on hand :				50,610	
Electricity Fund	.	.		12,000	
Petty Cash in hand :					
Borough Fund	.	.	25		
Electricity Fund	.	.	100		
Suspense Account :				125	
Borough Fund	.	.		465	
Exchequer Contribution A/c :					
Borough Fund	.	.		3,700	
Cash in hand :					
Mortgage Loans Fund	.			5,025	
					71,925
					£892,425

APPENDIX F.

GENERAL DISTRICT RATE.

SUMMARY OF ESTIMATE OF AMOUNT TO BE RAISED.

Committee.	Actual 1944-1945.	Estimate 1945-1946.	Estimate Actual to 31st Mar., 1946.	Estimate 1946-1947.
	£	£	£	£
Finance . . .	48,322	25,362	24,793	35,233
General Purposes .	7,353	10,425	10,649	11,880
Public Lighting .	12,904	18,590	16,839	22,300
Public Health . .	41,155	53,525	58,027	66,324
Roads . . .	78,279	121,509	134,724	145,676
Sewage Farms . .	21,732	23,424	20,544	27,556
Street Improvements, Town Planning, etc.	9,006	9,355	12,536	14,544
	218,751	262,190	278,112	323,513

Less—
Actual Surplus at 31st March, 1945 . 26,492

Net amount chargeable against Rate to
31st March, 1946 251,620

Estimated produce of current rate at
5s. 1d. to 31st March, 1946 . . 263,750

Estimated Surplus at 31st March, 1946 . ——— 12,130

Amount to be raised by rate for year to
31st March, 1947 . . . . £311,383

Estimated Assessable Value of General District Rate : £1,069,577.
1d. in the £ will produce £4,324 net.
6s. in the £ is equivalent to £311,328.

INDEX

119

Printed by Sir Isaac Pitman & Sons, Ltd., Bath, England
W—(1763)

PITMAN'S
BUSINESS HANDBOOKS

AN ABRIDGED LIST OF PRACTICAL GUIDES FOR
:: BUSINESS MEN AND ADVANCED STUDENTS ::

COMPLETE LIST OF COMMERCIAL BOOKS POST FREE ON APPLICATION

BOOK-KEEPING AND ACCOUNTS

ADVANCED ACCOUNTS. A Manual of Advanced Book-keeping and Accountancy for Accountants, Book-keepers and Business Men. Edited by ROGER N. CARTER, M.Com., F.C.A., *Lecturer on Accounting at the University of Manchester.* In demy 8vo, cloth gilt, 988 pp., 10s. 6d. net.

AUDITING, ACCOUNTING AND BANKING. By FRANK DOWLER, A.C.A. and E. MARDINOR HARRIS, *Associate of the Institute of Bankers.* In demy 8vo, cloth gilt, 328 pp., 7s. 6d. net.

THE PRINCIPLES OF AUDITING. A Practical Manual for Advanced Students and Practitioners. By F. R. M. DE PAULA (*of the firm of De Paula, Turner, Lake & Co.*), F.C.A. In demy 8vo, cloth gilt, 224 pp., 7s. 6d. net.

ACCOUNTANCY. By F. W. PIXLEY, F.C.A., *Barrister-at-Law, Ex-President of the Institute of Chartered Accountants.* In demy 8vo, cloth gilt, 318 pp., 7s. 6d. net.

AUDITORS : THEIR DUTIES AND RESPONSIBILITIES. By the same Author. Eleventh Edition. In demy 8vo, cloth gilt, 732 pp., 21s. net.

COST ACCOUNTS in Principle and Practice. By A. CLIFFORD RIDGWAY, F.C.A. In demy 8vo, cloth gilt, with 40 specially prepared forms, 5s. net.

COMPANY ACCOUNTS. By ARTHUR COLES, F.C.I.S. With a Preface by CHARLES COMINS, F.C.A. In demy 8vo, cloth gilt, 356 pp., 7s. 6d. net.

DICTIONARY OF BOOK-KEEPING. By R. J. PORTERS. In demy 8vo, 780 pp., 7s. 6d. net.

MANUFACTURING BOOK-KEEPING AND COSTS. By GEORGE JOHNSON, F.C.I.S. In demy 8vo, cloth gilt, 120 pp., 5s. net.

GOLD MINE ACCOUNTS AND COSTING. A Practical Manual for Officials, Accountants, Book-keepers, etc. By G. W. TAIT. In demy 8vo, cloth gilt, 5s. net.

THE ACCOUNTS OF EXECUTORS, ADMINISTRATORS AND TRUSTEES. With a Summary of the Law in so far as it relates to Accounts. By WILLIAM B. PHILLIPS, A.C.A. (Hons. Inter. and Final), A.C.I.S. Fourth Edition, Revised. In demy 8vo, cloth gilt, 150 pp., 5s. net.

PRACTICAL BOOK-KEEPING. By GEO. JOHNSON, F.C.I.S. In crown 8vo, cloth, 420 pp., 6s. net.

RAILWAY ACCOUNTS AND FINANCE. Railway Companies (Accounts and Returns) Act, 1911. By ALLEN E. NEWHOOK, A.K.C. In demy 8vo, cloth gilt, 148 pp., 5s. net.

DEPRECIATION AND WASTING ASSETS, and their treatment in computing annual profit and loss. By P. D. LEAKE, F.C.A. In demy 8vo, cloth gilt, 257 pp., 12s. 6d. net

ACCOUNTING. By S. S. Dawson, F.C.A. and R. C. De Zouche, F.C.A. In demy 8vo, cloth gilt, 290 pp., **10s. 6d.** net.

MANUAL OF COST ACCOUNTS. By Julius Lunt, A.C.A. (Hons.). In demy 8vo, cloth gilt, 124 pp., **6s.** net.

BUSINESS TRAINING

LECTURES ON BRITISH COMMERCE, including Finance, Insurance, Business and Industry. By the Rt. Hon. Frederick Huth Jackson, G. Armitage-Smith, M.A., D.Lit., Robert Bruce, C.B., Sir Douglas Owen, W. E. Barling, J. J. Bisgood, B.A., Allan Greenwell, F.G.S., James Graham. With a Preface by the Hon. W. Pember Reeves. In demy 8vo, cloth gilt, 295 pp., **7s. 6d.** net.

THE THEORY AND PRACTICE OF COMMERCE. Being a Complete Guide to Methods and Machinery of Business. Edited by F. Heelis, F.C.I.S., Assisted by Specialist Contributors. In demy 8vo, cloth gilt, 620 pp., with many facsimile forms, **6s.** net. Also in 2 vols.,each, price **3s. 6d.** net.

THE PRINCIPLES AND PRACTICE OF COMMERCE. By James Stephenson, M.A., M.Com., B.Sc. In demy 8vo, cloth gilt, 650 pp., with many facsimile forms, **10s. 6d.** net.

THE PRINCIPLES AND PRACTICE OF COMMERCIAL CORRESPONDENCE. By the same Author. In demy 8vo, 320 pp., **7s. 6d.** net.

THE PRINCIPLES OF COMMERCIAL HISTORY. By the same Author. In demy 8vo, 279 pp., **7s. 6d.** net.

THE PRINCIPLES AND PRACTICE OF COMMERCIAL ARITHMETIC. By P. W. Norris, M.A., B.Sc. (Hons.). In demy 8vo, 452 pp., **7s. 6d.** net.

MODERN BUSINESS AND ITS METHODS. A Manual of Business Organization, Management and Office Procedure for Commercial Students and Business Men. By W. Campbell, *Chartered Secretary*. In crown 8vo, cloth, 493 pp., **7s. 6d.** net. Also in 2 vols., each **3s. 6d.** net.

INSURANCE

INSURANCE. A Practical Exposition for the Student and Business Man. By T. E. Young, B.A., F.R.A.S. With a Practical Section on Workmen's Compensation Insurance, by W. R. Strong, F.I.A.; and the National Insurance Scheme, by Vyvyan Marr, F.F.A., F.I.A. Third Edition. Revised and Enlarged. In demy 8vo, cloth gilt, 440 pp., **10s. 6d.** net.

INSURANCE OFFICE ORGANISATION, MANAGEMENT, AND ACCOUNTS. By T. E. Young, B.A., F.R.A.S., and Richard Masters, A.C.A. Second Edition, Revised. In demy 8vo, cloth gilt, 150 pp., **5s.** net.

TALKS ON INSURANCE LAW. By Jos. A. Watson, B.Sc., LL.B. In crown 8vo, cloth, 140 pp., **5s.** net.

ORGANISATION AND MANAGEMENT

OFFICE ORGANISATION AND MANAGEMENT. Including Secretarial Work. By Lawrence R. Dicksee, M.Com., F.C.A., and H. E. Blain. *Late Tramways Manager, County Borough of West Ham.* Fourth Edition, Revised. In demy 8vo, cloth gilt, 314 pp., **7s. 6d.** net.

COUNTING HOUSE AND FACTORY ORGANISATION. A Practical Manual of Modern Methods applied to the Counting House and Factory. By J. Gilmour Williamson. In demy 8vo, cloth gilt, 182 pp., **6s. net.**

PITMAN'S BUSINESS HANDBOOKS

FILING SYSTEMS. Their Principles and their Application to Moderi Office Requirements. By EDWARD A. COPE. In crown 8vo, cloth gilt 200 pp. with illustrations, 2s. 6d. net.

INDUSTRIAL TRAFFIC MANAGEMENT. By GEO. B. LISSENDEN, *Autho of "Railway (Rebates) Case Law," etc., etc.* With a Foreword by CHARLE E. MUSGRAVE, *Secretary, London Chamber of Commerce.* In demy 8vo cloth gilt, 260 pp., 7s. 6d. net.

MOTOR ROAD TRANSPORT FOR COMMERCIAL PURPOSES. By JOH PHILLIMORE. With an Introduction by SIR H. P. MAYBURY, K.C.M.G C.B. In demy 8vo, cloth gilt, 216 pp., 12s. 6d. net.

THE PSYCHOLOGY OF MANAGEMENT. By L. M. GILBRETH. In demy 8vo, 354 pp., 7s. 6d. net.

EMPLOYMENT MANAGEMENT. Compiled and edited by DANIE BLOOMFIELD. In demy 8vo, 507 pp., 8s. 6d. net.

LECTURES ON INDUSTRIAL ADMINISTRATION. Edited by B. MUSCIO M.A. In crown 8vo, cloth, 276 pp., 6s. net.

OUTLINES OF INDUSTRIAL ADMINISTRATION. By R. O. HERFORD H. T. HILDAGE, and H. G. JENKINS. In demy 8vo, cloth gilt, 124 pp. 6s. net.

INDUSTRIAL CONTROL. By F. M. LAWSON. In demy 8vo, cloth gilt 130 pp., 8s. 6d. net.

MUNICIPAL OFFICE ORGANISATION AND MANAGEMENT. Edited b WILLIAM BATESON, A.C.A., F.S.A.A. With contributions by eminen authorities on Municipal Work and Practice. In crown 4to, half-leathe gilt, with about 250 diagrams and forms, 503 pp., 25s. net.

CLUBS AND THEIR MANAGEMENT. By FRANCIS W. PIXLEY, F.C.A. *Barrister-at-Law.* In demy 8vo, cloth gilt, 240 pp., 7s. 6d. net.

SOLICITOR'S OFFICE ORGANISATION, MANAGEMENT, AND ACCOUNTS By E. A. COPE and H. W. H. ROBINS. In demy 8vo, cloth gilt, 176 pp. with numerous forms, 5s. net.

COLLIERY OFFICE ORGANISATION AND ACCOUNTS. By J. W. INNES F.C.A., and T. COLIN CAMPBELL, F.C.I. In demy 8vo, 6s. net.

DRAPERY BUSINESS ORGANISATION AND MANAGEMENT. By J ERNEST BAYLEY. In demy 8vo, cloth gilt, 300 pp., 7s. 6d. net.

GROCERY BUSINESS ORGANISATION AND MANAGEMENT. By C. L. T BEECHING. With Chapters on Buying a Business, Grocers' Office Wor and Book-keeping, etc., by J. A. SMART. Second Edition. In demy 8vo cloth, 160 pp., 6s. net.

THE HISTORY, LAW, AND PRACTICE OF THE STOCK EXCHANGE. B A. P. POLEY, B.A. *Barrister-at-Law;* and F. H. CARRUTHERS GOULD Third Edition, revised. In demy 8vo, cloth gilt, 348 pp., 7s. 6d. net.

SHIPPING

SHIPPING OFFICE ORGANISATION, MANAGEMENT, AND ACCOUNTS A comprehensive Guide to the innumerable details connected with th Shipping Trade. By ALFRED CALVERT. In demy 8vo, cloth gilt, 203 pp. with numerous forms, 6s. net.

THE EXPORTER'S HANDBOOK AND GLOSSARY. By F. M. DUDENEY Foreword by W. EGLINGTON, *Founder and Editor of "The British Expo Gazette.'* In demy 8vo, cloth gilt, 254 pp. 6s. net.

THE PRINCIPLES OF MARINE LAW. (*See p. 7.*)

CASE AND FREIGHT COSTS. The Principles of Calculation relating to th Cost of, and Freight on, Sea or Commercial Cases. By A. W. E. CROSFIELD In crown 8vo, cloth, 62 pp., 2s. net.

BANKING AND FINANCE

MONEY, EXCHANGE AND BANKING, in their Practical, Theoretical, and Legal Aspects. A complete Manual for Bank Officials, Business Men, and Students of Commerce. By H. T. EASTON, *Associate of the Institute of Bankers.* Second Edition, Revised. In demy 8vo, cloth gilt, 312 pp., 6s. net.

FOREIGN EXCHANGE AND FOREIGN BILLS IN THEORY AND IN PRACTICE. By W. F. SPALDING, *Certificated Associate, Institute of Bankers, etc., etc.* Third Edition. In demy 8vo, cloth gilt, 227 pp., 7s. 6d. net.

EASTERN EXCHANGE, CURRENCY AND FINANCE. By the same Author. Third Edition. In demy 8vo, cloth, 375 pp., with 1 coloured and 6 black-and-white full-page plates, 15s. net.

FOREIGN EXCHANGE, A PRIMER OF. By the same Author. In crown 8vo, cloth, 108 pp., 3s. 6d. net.

PRACTICAL BANKING. By J. F. G. BAGSHAW, *Certificated Associate of the Institute of Bankers.* With chapters on "The Principles of Currency," by C. F. HANNAFORD, *Associate of the Institute of Bankers,* and "Bank Book-keeping," by W. H. PEARD, *Member of the Institute of Bankers in Ireland.* In demy 8vo, cloth gilt, 397 pp., 7s. 6d. net.

BANK ORGANISATION, MANAGEMENT, AND ACCOUNTS. By J. F. DAVIS, D.Lit., M.A., LL.B. (Lond.). In demy 8vo, cloth gilt, 165 pp., 6s. net

BILLS, CHEQUES, AND NOTES. A Handbook for Business Men and Lawyers. Together with the Bills of Exchange Act, 1882, the Amending Act, Bills of Exchange (Crossed Cheques) Act, 1906, and the Bills of Exchange (Time of Noting) Act, 1917. By J. A. SLATER, B.A., LL.B. Lond.). Third Edition. In demy 8vo, cloth gilt, 214 pp., 6s. net.

BANKERS' SECURITIES AGAINST ADVANCES. By LAWRENCE A. FOGG, *Certificated Associate of the Institute of Bankers.* In demy 8vo, cloth gilt, 120 pp. 6s. net.

BANKERS' ADVANCES. By F. R. STEAD. Edited by SIR JOHN PAGET, K.C. In demy 8vo, cloth, 144 pp., 6s. net.

THE EVOLUTION OF THE MONEY MARKET (1385-1915). An Historical and Analytical Study of the Rise and Development of Finance as a Centralised, Co-ordinated Force. By ELLIS T. POWELL, LL.B. (Lond.), D.Sc. (Econ., Lond.), *Barrister-at-Law.* In demy 8vo, cloth gilt, 748 pp., 10s. 6d. net.

SIMPLE INTEREST TABLES. By SIR WM. SCHOOLING, K,B.E. In crown 8vo, cloth gilt, 188 pp., 21s. net.

TALKS ON BANKING TO BANK CLERKS. By HAROLD E. EVANS, *Certificated Associate of the Institute of Bankers.* In crown 8vo, cloth, 152 pp., 2s. 6d. net.

DICTIONARY OF BANKING. A Complete Encyclopaedia of Banking Law and Practice. By W. THOMSON, *Bank Inspector.* Third Edition, Revised and Enlarged 1919. In crown 4to, half-leather gilt, 642 pp., 30s. net.

SECRETARIAL WORK

THE COMPANY SECRETARY'S VADE MECUM. Edited by PHILIP TOVEY, F.C.I.S. Third Edition. In foolscap 8vo, cloth, 3s. 6d. net.

SECRETARY'S HANDBOOK. A Practical Guide to the Work and Duties in connection with the Position of Secretary to a Member of Parliament, a Country Gentleman with a landed estate, a Charitable Institution, with a section devoted to the work of a Lady Secretary and a chapter dealing with Secretarial work in general. Edited by H. E. BLAIN, C.B.E. In demy 8vo, cloth gilt, 168 pp., 6s. net.

GUIDE FOR THE COMPANY SECRETARY. A Practical Manual and Work of Reference for the Company Secretary. By ARTHUR COLES, F.C.I.S. Second Edition, Enlarged and thoroughly Revised. With 76 facsimile forms, and the full text of the Companies Acts, 1908 and 1913, the Companies Clauses Act, 1845, Companies (Foreign Interest) Act, 1917, Companies (Particulars as to Directors) Act, 1917, and War Legislation. In demy 8vo, cloth gilt, 432 pp., 6s. net.

COMPANY ACCOUNTS. By the same Author. (See p. 1.)

DICTIONARY OF SECRETARIAL LAW AND PRACTICE. A Comprehensive Encyclopaedia of Information and Direction on all matters connected with the work of a Company Secretary. Fully illustrated with the necessary forms and documents. With Sections on special branches of Secretarial Work. Edited by PHILIP TOVEY, F.C.I.S. With contributions by nearly 40 eminent authorities on Company Law and Secretarial Practice, including : The Rt. Hon. G. N. Barnes, M.P.; F. Gore-Browne, K.C., M.A.; A. Crew, F.C.I.S.; J. P. Earnshaw, F.C.I.S.; M. Webster Jenkinson, F.C.A.; F. W. Pixley, F.C.A. Third Edition, enlarged and revised. In one volume, cloth gilt, 1011 pp., 42s. net.

THE TRANSFER OF STOCKS, SHARES, AND OTHER MARKETABLE SECURITIES. A Manual of the Law and Practice. By F. D. HEAD, B.A. (Oxon.), *Barrister-at-Law.* Second Edition, Revised and Enlarged. In demy 8vo, cloth gilt, 220 pp., 5s. net.

THE CHAIRMAN'S MANUAL. Being a guide to the management of meetings in general, and of meetings of local authorities, with separate and complete treatment of the meetings of public companies. By GURDON PALIN, *Barrister-at-Law.* and ERNEST MARTIN, F.C.I.S. In crown 8vo, cloth gilt, 192 pp., 3s. 6d. net.

HOW TO TAKE MINUTES. Edited by ERNEST MARTIN, F.C.I.S. Second Edition, Revised and Enlarged. In demy 8vo, cloth gilt, 130 pp., 2s. 6d. net.

WHAT IS THE VALUE OF A SHARE ? Tables for readily and correctly ascertaining (1) the present value of shares ; and (2) what dividends should be paid annually to justify the purchase or market price of shares. By D. W. ROSSITER. In demy 8vo, limp cloth. 20 pp., 2s. 6d. net.

PROSPECTUSES : HOW TO READ AND UNDERSTAND THEM. By PHILIP TOVEY, F.C.I.S. In demy 8vo, cloth, 109 pp., 5s. net.

INCOME TAX

INCOME TAX AND SUPER-TAX PRACTICE. Incorporating the Consolidation Act of 1918 and the Finance Acts, 1919 and 1920. Fourth Edition. By W. E. SNELLING. In demy 8vo, cloth gilt, 15s. net.

INCOME TAX AND SUPER-TAX LAW AND CASES. A Practical Exposition of the Law, for the use of Income Tax Officials, Solicitors, Accountants, etc. Fourth Edition (in the press). By W. E. SNELLING.

COAL MINES EXCESS PAYMENTS, Guarantee Payments and Levies for Closed Mines. By W. E. SNELLING. Demy 8vo, cloth gilt, 176 pp., 12s. 6d. net.

EXCESS PROFITS (Including Excess Mineral Rights) DUTY, and Levies under the Munitions of War Acts. Incorporating the Provisions of the Income Tax Acts made applicable by Statute and by Regulation, the provisions of the Finance Act, 1920, and also the Regulations of the Commissioners of Inland Revenue, and of the Minister of Munitions. By W. E. SNELLING. Sixth Edition, Revised and Enlarged. In demy 8vo, cloth gilt, 516 pp., **21s.** net.

SUPER TAX TABLES. By G. O. PARSONS. 16 pp., **1s.** net.

ECONOMICS

ECONOMIC GEOGRAPHY. By J. McFARLANE, M.A., M.Com. In demy 8vo, cloth gilt, 568 pp., with 18 illustrations, **10s. 6d.** net

THE PRINCIPLES OF ECONOMIC GEOGRAPHY. By R. N. RUDMOSE BROWN, D.Sc., *Lecturer in Geography in the University of Sheffield.* In demy 8vo, cloth gilt, 223 pp., **10s. 6d.** net.

OUTLINES OF THE ECONOMIC HISTORY OF ENGLAND. A Study in Social Development. By H. O. MEREDITH, M.A., M Com., *Fellow of King's College, Cambridge.* In demy 8vo, cloth gilt, 376 PP., **7s. 6d.** net

THE HISTORY AND ECONOMICS OF TRANSPORT. By ADAM W. KIRKALDY, M.A., B.Litt., Oxford; M.Com., Birmingham; and ALFRED DUDLEY EVANS. In demy 8vo, cloth gilt, 348 pp., **15s.** net.

THE ECONOMICS OF TELEGRAPHS AND TELEPHONES. By JOHN LEE, M.A., *Traffic Manager, Post Office Telegraphs.* In crown 8vo, cloth gilt, 92 pp., **2s. 6d.** net.

INDUSTRY AND FINANCE. (Supplementary Volume.) Edited by ADAM W. KIRKALDY, M.A., B.Litt., M.Com. Deals with the results of inquiries arranged by the Section of Economic Science and Statistics of the British Association. In demy 8vo, cloth, **5s.** net.

TALKS WITH WORKERS. On Wealth, Wages and Production. In crow 8vo., 124 pp,, limp cloth, **2s.** net.

ADVERTISING AND SALESMANSHIP

THE CRAFT OF SILENT SALESMANSHIP. A Guide to Advertisemen Construction. By C. MAXWELL TREGURTHA and J. W. FRINGS. Size 6¼ in. by 9¼ in., cloth, 98 pp., with illustrations. **5s.** net.

THE NEW BUSINESS. A Handbook dealing with the Principles of Adver tising, Selling, and Marketing. By HARRY TIPPER, *President, Advertisin Men's League, New York.* In demy 8vo, cloth gilt, 406 pp., **8s. 6d.** net.

SALESMANSHIP. By W A. CORBION and G. E. GRIMSDALE. In crowr 8vo, cloth, 186 pp.. **2s. 6d.** net.

PRACTICAL SALESMANSHIP. By N. C. FOWLER, Junr. In crown 8vo 337 pp., **7s. 6d.** net.

COMMERCIAL TRAVELLING. By ALBERT E. BULL. In crown 8vo, clotl gilt, 174 pp., **3s. 6d.** net.

THEORY AND PRACTICE OF ADVERTISING. By W. DILL SCOTT, PH.D In large crown 8vo, cloth, with 61 illustrations, 240 pp., **7s. 6d.** net.

THE PSYCHOLOGY OF ADVERTISING. By the same Author. In larg crown 8vo, cloth, with 67 illustrations, 282 pp., **7s. 6d.** net.

ADVERTISING AS A BUSINESS FORCE. By P. T. CHERINGTON. In dem 8vo, cloth, 586 pp., **8s. 6d.** net.

HOW TO ADVERTISE. By G. FRENCH, *Editor of the "Advertising News.'* In crown 8vo., **8s. 6d.** net.

THE MANUAL OF SUCCESSFUL STOREKEEPING. By W. A. HOTCHKIN In demy 3vo, 298 pp., **8s. 6d,** net.

ADS. AND SALES. By Herbert N. Casson. In demy 8vo, cloth, 167 pp. 8s. 6d. net.

THE PRINCIPLES OF PRACTICAL PUBLICITY. By Truman A. de Weese. In large crown 8vo, cloth, with 43 illustrations, 266 pp., 7s. 6d. net.

LAW

MERCANTILE LAW. By J. A. Slater, B.A., LL.B. A practical exposition for Law Students, Business Men, and Advanced Classes in Commercial Colleges and Schools. Fourth Edition. In demy 8vo, cloth gilt, 464 pp., 7s. 6d. net.

COMPANIES AND COMPANY LAW. Together with the Companies (Consolidation) Act, 1908, and the Act of 1913. By A. C. Connell, LL.B. (Lond.), *of the Middle Temple, Barrister-at-Law.* Second Edition, Revised. In demy 8vo, cloth gilt, 348 pp., 6s. net.

COMPANY CASE LAW. By F. D. Head, B.A. (Oxon.), *Barrister-at-Law.* In demy 8vo, cloth gilt, 314 pp., 7s. 6d. net.

THE LAW OF CARRIAGE. By J. E. R. Stephens, B.A., *of the Middle Temple, Barrister-at-Law.* In demy 8vo, cloth gilt, 340 pp., 5s. net.

THE LAW RELATING TO THE CARRIAGE BY LAND OF PASSENGERS, ANIMALS, AND GOODS. By S. W. Clarke, *Barrister-at-Law.* In demy 8vo, cloth gilt, 350 pp., 7s. 6d. net.

INCOME TAX AND SUPER-TAX LAW AND CASES. (See p. 5.)

THE LAW RELATING TO SECRET COMMISSIONS AND BRIBES (Christmas Boxes, Gratuities, Tips, etc.) ; The Prevention of Corruption Acts, 1906 and 1916. By Albert Crew, *Barrister-at-Law ; Lee Prizeman o Gray's Inn.* Second Edition. In demy 8vo, cloth gilt, 252 pp., 10s. 6d. net.

BANKRUPTCY, DEEDS OF ARRANGEMENT, AND BILLS OF SALE. By W. Valentine Ball, M.A., and G. Mills, B.A., *Barristers-at-Law.* Third Edition, Revised in accordance with the Bankruptcy and the Deeds of Arrangement Acts, 1914. In demy 8vo, 364 pp., 5s. net.

PRINCIPLES OF MARINE LAW. By Lawrence Duckworth, *Barrister-at-Law.* Third Edition, Revised. In demy 8vo, about 400 pp., 7s. 6d. net.

GUIDE TO THE LAW OF LICENSING. The Handbook for all Licence-holders. By J. Wells Thatcher, *Barrister-at-Law.* In demy 8vo, cloth gilt, 200 pp., 5s. net.

RAILWAY (REBATES) CASE LAW. By Geo. B. Lissenden. In demy 8vo, cloth gilt, 450 pp., 10s. 6d. net.

PARTNERSHIP LAW AND ACCOUNTS. By R. W. Holland, O.B.E., M.A., M.Sc., LL.D., *Barrister-at-Law.* In demy 8vo, cloth gilt, 159 pp. 6s. net.

THE LAW OF CONTRACT. By the same author. In demy 8vo, cloth 123 pp., 5s. net.

THE LAW RELATING TO THE CHILD : Its Protection, Education, an Employment. With Introduction on the Laws of Spain, Germany France and Italy ; and Bibliography. By the same author. In dem 8vo, 166 pp., 5s. net.

GUIDE TO THE REGISTRATION OF BUSINESS NAMES ACT, 1916. B Kenneth Brown, *Solicitor.* In crown 8vo, paper boards, 1s. net.

CONVEYANCING. By E. A. Cope. In crown 8vo, cloth, 206 pp., 3s. 6d. net

WILLS, EXECUTORS, AND TRUSTEES. By J. A. Slater, B.A., LL.B With a chapter on Intestacy. In foolscap 8vo, cloth, 122 pp., 2s. 6d. net

INHABITED HOUSE DUTY. By W. E. Snelling. In demy 8vo, clot gilt, 356 pp., 12s. 6d. net.

THE LAW OF REPAIRS AND DILAPIDATIONS. By T. Cato Worsfold M.A., LL.D. In crown 8vo, cloth gilt, 104 pp., **3s. 6d.** net.

THE LAW OF EVIDENCE. By W. Nembhard Hibbert, LL.D. *Barrister at-Law.* Third Edition, Revised. In crown 8vo, 120 pp., **7s. 6d.** net.

THE LAW OF PROCEDURE. By the same Author. In demy 8vo, cloth gilt, 122 pp., **5s.** net.

BILLS, CHEQUES, AND NOTES. (See page 4.)

THE HISTORY, LAW, AND PRACTICE OF THE STOCK EXCHANGE (See page 3.)

BUSINESS REFERENCE BOOKS

BUSINESS MAN'S ENCYCLOPAEDIA AND DICTIONARY OF COMMERCE A reliable and comprehensive work of reference on all commercial subjects specially designed and written for the busy merchant, the commercia student, and the modern man of affairs. Edited by J. A. Slater, B.A. LL.B. (Lond.) Assisted by upwards of 50 specialists as contributors With numerous maps, illustrations, facsimile business forms and lega documents, diagrams, etc. In 4 vols., large crown 4to (each 450 pp.) cloth gilt, £4 4s. 0d. net.

BUSINESS MAN'S GUIDE. Seventh Revised Edition. With French, German Spanish and Italian equivalents for the Commercial Words and Terms Edited by J. A. Slater, B.A., LL.B. (Lond.). The work includes ove 2,000 articles. In crown 8vo, cloth, 520 pp., **6s. 6d.** net.

COMMERCIAL ARBITRATIONS. By E. J. Parry, B.Sc., F.I.C., F.C.S An invaluable guide to business men who are called upon to conduc arbitrations. In crown 8vo, cloth gilt, **3s. 6d.** net.

PERSONAL EFFICIENCY IN BUSINESS. By E. E. Purington. In crow 8vo, cloth gilt, 341 pp., **7s. 6d.** net.

DICTIONARY OF COMMERCIAL CORRESPONDENCE IN SEVEN LAN GUAGES: ENGLISH, FRENCH, GERMAN, SPANISH, ITALIAN PORTUGUESE AND RUSSIAN. In demy 8vo, cloth, 718 pp., **12s. 6d.** net Third Edition.

A MANUAL OF DUPLICATING METHODS By W. Desborough. I demy 8vo, cloth, 90 pp., illustrated, **2s. 6d.** net.

COMMON COMMODITIES AND INDUSTRIES SERIES. Each book i crown 8vo, cloth, illustrated, **3s.** net. Volumes already published o Tea, Coffee, Sugar, Oils, Wheat, Rubber, Iron and Steel, Copper, Coa Timber, Cotton, Silk, Wool, Linen, Tobacco, Leather, Clays, Paper, Soaj Glass, Gums and Resins, The Motor Industry, Boot and Shoe Industry, Ga and Gas Making, Petroleum, Salt, Furniture, Coal Tar, Knitted Fabric Zinc, Asbestos, Photography, Silver, Carpets, Paints and Varnishes, Cordag and Cordage Hemp and Fibres, Acids and Alkalis, Gold, Electricity, Butte and Cheese, Aluminium, The British Corn Trade, Engraving, Lead, Stone and Quarries, Clothing Trades Industry, Modern Explosives, Electri Lamp Industry, Perfumery, Ice and Cold Storage, Telegraphy Telephon and Wireless.

BUSINESS ORGANISATION AND MANAGEMENT.
A Monthly Magazine of High Standard for Business Men.
Price **1s. 6d.** Post Free, **1s. 9d.** Annual Subscription **18s.**

COMPLETE LIST POST FREE ON APPLICATION

Sir Isaac Pitman & Sons, Ltd., Parker Street, Kingsway, W.C.
And at Bath, Melbourne, Toronto and New York

CPSIA information can be obtained
at www.ICGtesting.com
Printed in the USA
BVHW051830051118
532208BV00022B/3772/P